led by Mind and Spirit

By the same authors and available from Mowbray/Continuum

Disturbed by Mind and Spirit: Mental Health and Healing in Parish Ministry – 9780826427755

Called by
Mind and Spirit

Crossing the Borderlands
of Childhood

Gavin Knight and
Joanna Knight

mowbray

Published by Mowbray, an imprint of the Continuum International
Publishing Group Ltd

The Tower Building   80 Maiden Lane
11 York Road   Suite 704
London   New York
SE1 7NX   NY 10038

www.continuumbooks.com

First published 2010

British Library Cataloguing-in-Publication Data
A catalogue record for this book is available from the British Library.

ISBN 9781441137616

Designed and typeset by Free Range Book Design & Production Ltd
Printed and bound by the MPG Books Group

We dedicate *Called by Mind and Spirit* to our children, Gabriel, Fabian and Theo, who have been ever-present pilgrims during the course of writing this book. Our love (and apologies) to them. These pages are also dedicated to all borderland children, in particular our godchildren, William, Robyn, Euan, Lydia, Olivia, Esther, Siena and Zacchary.

Contents

Acknowledgements

Our particular thanks go to Dallin Vines whose four poems were written specifically for the book's purpose. We would like to thank Keith Denerley and Michael Tavinor for their time and trouble spent reading the manuscript and all their comments, greatly appreciated. We would also like to acknowledge those individuals whose writing has influenced the book in particular, namely: Jerome Berryman, Esther de Waal, Christopher Jamison, Timothy Radcliffe and Rowan Williams.

This book has been written from the specific borderland context of Monmouth. We would therefore like to thank both Monmouth School and Ty Mawr Convent which have helped inspire and influence much of the material here.

Authors' note

After much deliberation, we have referred to the child as 'he' throughout as 'she' created clashes in the text and 'he'/'she' made for awkward reading in places. For similar reasons, we have sometimes used 'parent' as a generic term of reference, and not always included specific references to the other parenting figures in children's lives.

Foreword by the Archbishop of Wales

Jesus had some pretty radical things to say about the children of his day, especially when compared to the prevailing views of most people in first-century Palestine. To his contemporaries, children were of value, not in their own right, but as those who would become so as they grew up because they could look after their parents in their old age. Their value, in other words, lay in the future, not the present. To Jesus, however, 'the kingdom of God belonged to such as these' (Mark 10:14). They were to be valued for their own sake and not for some future utilitarian purpose. They deserved as much respect as any other person, for children as well as adults were made in God's image. Therefore Jesus invited children to come to him and said that 'whoever received a child in his name received him' (Matthew 18: 2–5).

Called by Mind and Spirit starts from this premise and, through theological and psychological insights, offers guidance to individuals, the Church and society in general to help nurture the well-being of children. It also outlines practical ways in which the Christian Church, through imaginative use of symbol and liturgy, can give space and welcome to children so that it can truly live out the Gospel. This involves, of course, far more than protecting children from harm. It is about loving, cherishing, valuing so that the haunting words of one of the victims of those children deported to Australia between the 1940s and 1967, 'I have never felt loved by anyone in my whole life,' need never be uttered again.

All of us – Christians as well as everyone else – have much to learn about children and childhood. We may not cause visible harm but we do bring them up in a world that places great value on material things and on stressing the rights of the individual as opposed to those of the community. There are many forces which hold children back but the Christian faith can help us be confident about our nurturing of them. What we have to do is to rediscover our heritage – this book helps us to do this.

The Most Reverend Dr Barry Morgan
Archbishop of Wales

There is a place we have not yet discovered. And yet, in our mind's eye, we have visited there again and again, working out its purpose, its parameters, its unlikely origins. When we speak of it, we do so tentatively, always somehow with an apology attached. It's hard to describe a place you have not found yet; to make believe a reality that apparently does not exist.

This is a borderland place. Its identity is as yet unrealized. Calling us back to our roots, it is at once connected and connecting,[1] located in a landscape we both know and do not know, dislocated from any real knowledge of how our vision might come about. And yet the vision speaks of things real enough: repentance, renewal and transformation. People will go there, not because they have to but because they choose to, prepared to risk both joy and pain, discomfort and wonder.

Over the years we have tried to run from our yearning, reminding ourselves of more sensible, realistic aspirations. But each time we try to run, carrying our children with us, we find ourselves drawing back, turning round, returning to the point where in fact we started out. Our identity is, and long since has been, bound up in this unknown vision. In time we hope it will shape and form us, that others will see it also and come to join us. It is, we hope, a place to which both we and others are travelling. Rightly or wrongly, we call this place Metanoia.

JDK

Introduction

I see borderlands as places where different cultures and histories meet and mix, perhaps challenge one another, and from which the new can then open up. And what I find in this outer landscape which is my home has also become true of the interior landscape, the inscape, which I culture and nurture.

(Esther de Waal, 2001)

Childhood is a borderland place. Within these borders lies the imagination, restless, seeking, unmoulded, and ripe for transformation. As adults, it can be all too easy to forget how we might cross these borders; to remain stuck somehow in the places in which we have grown comfortable, coveting perhaps our own experience or, more passive yet, simply ceasing to notice the journeys our children are making. Years, decades even, might have passed since we felt able to explore the parameters that now confine us. But the opportunity to revisit and explore the borderlands that once informed our journey is still available: first, through an understanding of ourselves and second, through an understanding of our children.

Borderlands are not places that encourage sentimentality. Their landscape is both constant and changing. Often marked by territories which have been fought over for generations, even centuries, these places of past unrest have switched identities back and forth with a high cost attached. While in the United Kingdom border territories are no longer places of violence, but rather represent barely visible lines 'no longer worth killing for' (Kroll, 2000, p. 3),

1

there is something deeply pervasive about borderland territory.[1] Since having moved to the border town of Monmouth in South Wales just four years ago, I am increasingly aware of the context I inhabit and of how this awareness is shared by many:

> From this awareness has risen a recognition that pilgrims on the Christian journey often enter border country. Political events, cultural changes and developments in science and technology are some of the stimuli that daily challenge us to apply a Christian mind to a fast-moving world. In our personal lives, an unexpected change can suddenly occur and we find ourselves in an unfamiliar landscape, unsure of which direction to take next.
> (Borderland Series Introduction, p. vii)[2]

Borderlands are, therefore, places whose historical, physical and geographical properties make powerful connections with our spiritual and emotional states. The chapters that follow will draw on this borderland imagery and apply it to an altogether different context, to the place of childhood itself.

A response to childhood today

In recent years, our understanding of what it is to be a child in twenty-first-century Britain has been constantly under review: by the government ('Every Child Matters', 2003), by key agencies (health, education and social services), by leading charities (e.g. NSPCC, UniCef and the Children's Society) and by the Church. At the heart of this understanding lies a deep-rooted concern about our children's well-being, physical, emotional and spiritual. This is no surprise given contemporary, very real anxieties about 'how the modern world is damaging our children' (Palmer, 2006). Child psychology has had an increased role to play in the debate on childhood ranging from television programmes such as Robert Winston's 'Child of our Time' and the government-commissioned report, 'The Byron Review: Children and New Technology'. Most recently, the high-profile publication of *The Good Childhood Inquiry: Social Values in a Competitive Age* (Layard and Dunn,

2009), sponsored by the Children's Society, has sparked renewed interest about the place of children in modern society.

'Excessive individualism' is the damning conclusion drawn by the Good Childhood Inquiry as to the cause of children's difficulties in Britain today. Uncompromising in its tenor, the indictment is not one we as adults can easily ignore. In its summary of the report, the message from the Children's Society is clear: 'Most of the obstacles children face today are linked to the belief among adults that the prime duty of the individual is to make the most of their own life, rather than contribute to the good of others.'[3] In other words, the importance of our relationships with one another appears to have been superseded, even fractured, by a desire to pursue self-interest above all else. The impact of this pursuit is wide-ranging, including: 'high family break up, teenage unkindness, commercial pressures towards premature sexualization, unprincipled advertising, too much competition in education, and acceptance of income inequality'. 'Excessive individualism' comes with a heavy price.

Not surprisingly, the Children's Society report produced a flurry of headlines: 'Selfish adults "damage childhood"' we were told by the BBC;[4] 'Be less selfish and don't split up,' wrote the *Church Times*;[5] 'The Children's Society Report should trouble us all,' wrote the *Daily Telegraph*.[6] And yet despite, or perhaps because of, the deeply uncomfortable, almost overwhelming nature of the report's outcome, it is all too tempting to distance ourselves from a debate which, whether we like it or not, is of relevance to us all. 'In short,' writes Rowan Williams in the Afterword, 'this report is telling us that adults have to change if children are to be better cared for and their welfare better secured' (2009, pp. 169–170).

While the report brings to public attention a thought-provoking thesis about childhood, it does little to place its conclusions within a theological framework. The omission was highlighted at the General Synod in July 2009:

> The Revd Professor Paul Fiddes (Baptist Union) said that the report did not reflect on the relationship of the child to God, even though the Good Childhood Inquiry spoke of the spiritual dimension. He wanted to see more about the theological foundations for the reasons why Christians should be concerned with the findings of the

Inquiry. He wanted to see more about the theology of growth in Christ. He would also like more about how growth in human relations could integrate with growth in God.[7]

The general thesis of this book – a belief in the vocation of all children – will consider just this, that is, 'the theology of growth in Christ' in relation to childhood today, and so address an important gap evident in the Good Childhood Inquiry.

Despite, however, any theological gaps in the report, it is evident that both the Children's Society and the Church are united in a desire to understand and value children better. The report's publication coincided with the thirtieth anniversary of the United Nations' International Year of the Child, originally formulated to highlight difficulties faced by children world-wide, including poverty, malnutrition and lack of access to education. In recognition of this anniversary, the Anglican Church designated 2009 as 'The Year of the Child', requesting churches of all denominations to mark the anniversary with 'a distinctive Christian contribution'.[8] This book will respond to the Church's request at two levels, theological and psychological, and, in doing so, bring together two critical aspects of thinking about childhood.

A shared response

From both a theological and psychological perspective, the Good Childhood Inquiry asks us as adults to engage in a *metanoia* experience: that is, to admit that we have done wrong, to make changes, to turn ourselves around and start again. The task is daunting, to say the least. Engagement in this task will mean something different for each individual that approaches it. Yet we should not be over-hasty in our rush to do, to act, to make changes. Honest soul-searching and self-reflection are the necessary tools with which we, as adults, need to equip ourselves before seeking to take things forward: 'Just being prepared to look at ourselves from a different perspective is already embracing change' (Wilde McCormick, 2008).

Erik Erikson, an eminent psychoanalyst writing in the middle of last century, understood the need for adults to consider themselves from a different perspective if they were successfully to engage in the process of 'establishing and guiding the next generation' (1950/1995, p. 240).[9] He viewed this process as a developmental stage, namely 'generativity', and held strong beliefs about the reasons which hindered a parent from achieving this stage for themselves:

> The reasons are often to be found in early childhood impressions; in excessive self-love based on a too strenuously self-made personality; and finally ... in the lack of some faith, some 'belief in the species', which would make a child appear to be a welcome trust of the community.
>
> (Erikson, 1950/1995, p. 240).

It strikes me that Erikson's concern about parenting nearly sixty years ago has much in common with the Good Childhood Inquiry's findings. Erikson's phrase 'a welcome trust of the community' resonates strongly with the Good Childhood Inquiry's desire for children to be viewed as 'a sacred trust' (Layard and Dunn, 2009, p. x).[10] The Good Childhood Inquiry, however, takes the issue even further. Laden with criticism about today's society, the report does not only cite an extensive list of the 'obstacles' of childhood, it also draws up a set of recommendations. Recommendations are divided into several categories, aimed at different agencies or bodies, specifically, parents, teachers, the government, the media, advertisers and, finally, 'all society'. The recommendations for parents are summarized as follows:

Parents should:
- Make a long-term commitment to each other.
- Be fully informed about what is involved before their child is born.
- Love their children, each other and establish boundaries for children.
- Help children develop spiritual qualities.

In a society in which consumerist images and short-term goals have become everyday tender, the recommendations provide a necessary, even visionary starting point. At one level, as a parent, clinical child psychologist and spouse of an Anglican priest, I can do nothing but endorse the recommendations set before me; at a more instinctive level, however, I long to alter the language somewhat, build into it a recognition of the enormity of each of these tasks, an awareness perhaps that, in order to bring people on board with this vision, we need to engage in continued debate, be prepared to come up against different values, different experiences, different aspirations, if we are to come to a shared understanding of our children at all. This commitment to dialogue, already begun by many, is no small task. As the report reminds us, it needs to happen at all levels: as parents, carers, teachers, institutions, as communities, both secular and faith-based, as society as a whole. Seeking to nurture a child's well-being is not the task of any one individual but is a community responsibility. Society needs to recognize where it is going wrong, to repent and set about both change and renewal. This is the context for the *metanoia* experience in childhood today.

A response to 'spiritual sloth'

A willingness to look at ourselves honestly and thoughtfully is not yet another platform for egocentric behaviour. On the contrary, the process demands both psychological and spiritual insight. This is borne out in clinical work with children and their families where, in order for parents or carers to engage in the therapeutic process, they need to be aware, firstly, that a problem exists and secondly, that their own beliefs and behaviour have a role to play in the child's presenting difficulties. Just as, therefore, some degree of psychological insight is necessary in a clinical context with children, so too a degree of spiritual insight is essential if we as adults are to foster our children's spirituality. A lack of insight can lead to one form of spiritual sloth, also known as *acedia*, and is discussed at length by Christopher Jamison in his book *Finding Happiness: Monastic Steps for a Fulfilling Life*:

spiritual carelessness seems to me to underlie much contemporary unhappiness in Western culture. The word [*acedia*] is no longer used not because the reality is obsolete but because we have stopped noticing it. We are too busy to be spiritually self-aware and our children grow up in a culture that suffers from collective *acedia*. *Acedia* has established itself so well that it is now part of modernity.

(Jamison, 2008, p. 57)

The idea that we have simply ceased to notice our *acedia* is deeply unsettling. Supporting this, it is notable that, despite a rising number of books and reports on children's spirituality,[11] by and large the public debate on childhood has remained primarily secular. There seems always to be a continued imbalance tipped towards a secular response to the challenges of modern childhood. This imbalance is indicative of the very *acedia* about which Christopher Jamison speaks so compellingly. In the landmark book, *Toxic Childhood: How the Modern World is Damaging Our Children and What We Can Do About It*, the index cites not one reference to spirituality or Christianity and only two references to religion in total, both of which, when examined, are negative.[12] In this kind of context, it is self-evident that the voice of the Church is frequently misrepresented, misunderstood and undervalued. The challenge remains how to marry more convincingly a psychological viewpoint with a theological one.

Aims and objectives

This book will offer a response to the *acedia* of our times by seeking to articulate a shared perspective of childhood, one which understands the journey of childhood to be sacred and which holds in mind our Christian heritage. Writing in alternate chapters (theology first, then psychology), we will begin by drawing on stories of our own heritage, both Christian and familial. For the remainder of the book, key themes of childhood – identity, formation and vocation – will be explored from the dual perspectives of theology and psychology. These themes are not seen as independent units but rather have many overlaps which help shape and inform one another. Our main aims and objectives are as follows:

- To bring to light a shared model of childhood, one rooted in both theological and psychological understanding.
- To consider how this model might inform an adult response to nurturing the whole child, in particular the child's spiritual formation.
- To translate this response into the context of those environments where the fostering of children's faith and Christian identity is central (e.g. our churches).
- To enable all those involved with children, be they carer, professional, lay or ordained, to reflect on their role as adults; to consider how their own ways of thinking and being might impact on the spiritual and emotional development of children today.

The sacramental rites of anointing and initiation (baptism, confirmation and ordination) provide the framework for the book's theological chapters. These rites, which represent thresholds to a new stage of spiritual life, are then used in the psychological chapters as a vehicle for reflecting on the main stages of childhood (infancy and early childhood, middle childhood and adolescence). In this way, psychological thinking about the developmental progression through childhood is guided by theological reflection and practice. These theological-psychological connections are, however, by no means literal or concrete. Quite clearly, baptism does not only take place in infancy and early childhood; confirmation is, at least in the Anglican Church, more common in adolescence than it is in 'middle childhood' (the years between four and eleven); and, as for ordination, this rite does not belong to childhood at all. However, while ordination is perhaps the least obvious rite to draw upon when exploring the place of childhood, its significance is central as it helps bring forward the idea of vocation to childhood itself.

In reshaping the boundaries of these rites of initiation and anointing, the book will explore how theological thinking might practically inform childhood today. In doing so, it will make tentative steps towards discerning how a more creative response to childhood might help us respond to twenty-first-century *acedia*, and better nurture not only children's sense of identity and formation but, underpinning these, their sense of vocation. While it is generally accepted that vocation is 'a term that applies to everyone – regardless of gender, race, class or age' (Bunge, 2008, p. 32), vocation as a theological concept has been largely omitted from discussions of childhood. Marcia Bunge's recent observation about the importance of understanding vocation in childhood is, therefore, a welcome arrival:

> Since theological understandings of vocation take into account large questions of meaning and purpose in life, and since they also value the particular roles and responsibilities in which individuals carry out their specific callings, exploring the vocation of the child is a particularly rich and fruitful way to challenge common and often narrow conceptions of children; to deepen our understanding of who children are and the significant roles they play in families and community life; and to strengthen our commitment to children in our own various and specific callings in life.
>
> (Bunge, 2008, p. 34)[13]

Vocation, like childhood, is multi-layered. What is more, it is not some fixed entity with a neat beginning, middle and end. If the roots of our vocation lie in the first throes of our sacred journey, then that pilgrimage surely began with life itself. As, in the narrative structure of this book, we cross the borderlands of childhood, each transition point (whether sacramental or developmental) will mark a frontier of its own. As we set out on our own journey, it is our hope that this book will be shaped by a theology of vocation: a shared belief in what it is to journey through childhood, to be called by God.

Joanna Knight, Lent 2009

Part 1

Who Do We Think We Are?

I Am a Story

I am a story
Written by hands that would
Weave me in wonder.
Faint footsteps print the map
Of my journey, tongue telling
Lone tales of adventure and pain.
Glass shadow, what are you,
Whose face do I see?
Timid traveller, flickering tale,
I am my story.

I am a history
Turn my pages you'll find
My father lifting me high,
Women's laughter, fire
Throwing its light on taut faces,
Hooves clattering steep cobbles
And long-ago weeping by
Windswept graves where primroses
Still promised the spring.
I am my history.

I am a people
Treading shared highways,
Running to unfurl the banners
That speak of our dreams,
Singing songs carved over
Centuries, catching hands held
In the dark times,
Counting our dead.
Fellow fortunes, tangled yearnings,
I am my people.

I am a pilgrimage,
Bound in the leaves of faith shared
Through lost seasons, their
Branches whispering to roots
Wrapped deep in the soil
Of my planting.
Faltering wayfarer, feeble follower,
I am my pilgrimage.

Dallin Vines

Chapter 1

Markings

Church spires are the great punctuation points of the ... countryside. But the religious buildings of this country not only tell where we are geographically, they tell us where we've come from. They're often the only place in a community which has a living, visible connection to the past. They hot-wire us into our history.[1]

Window-gazing

The church in which I grew up was, and still is, rather solid and unpretentious. Like the town in which it is located, the church is Victorian, built for purpose and permanence. Today, the church is anchored on an island of busy streets, empty offices and newly erected flats. Despite its lacklustre situation, as a child I was captivated by the scale and grandeur of this place of welcome. The internal features were no less imposing, bolstered by the starkness of the liturgical structures. The warm familiarity of the community became the context for my spirit's growth and development.

It was during the lengthy sermons that my attention would wander. In particular, I remember my gaze would fix upon the windows adjacent to the 'family' pew. I flitted from window to window. Keen to help time pass, I imagined being a participant in the stained-glass scenes before me. The images of Jesus, Mary and the disciples crafted onto the translucent glass became the characters in an imaginary drama, a drama in which I would lose myself through its potentialities and possibilities. What would it be like to meet Jesus? Where might he lead me?

The windows attracted me like a life-size picture book. Each atmospheric scene conveyed a love which, as a small boy, I could not begin to describe. This was my own private retreat. With a child's ability to transcend all boundaries of imagination and faith, I met Jesus at these improbable times and I kept meeting him on different occasions. I accompanied him out of the wilderness; I travelled with him as he joined his family and friends; I walked through the city and the countryside with his many followers. It was in this picture book that I started to ask questions about my identity before God. I had started to cross the borderlands.

Roots

'Who do you think you are?' is one of the most popular current series on BBC television. After seven series to date, this award-winning programme has captured the imagination of a nation. The concept behind the programme is a simple one – to investigate the family tree of a given celebrity. The search back in time reveals some fascinating insights into social, political and religious history spanning various centuries and, invariably, different continents. The genealogical narratives of the celebrity subjects are scrutinized by millions of armchair viewers. The popular success of the programme has gone hand in hand with an upsurge in people's investigation of their family histories. Specially designed computer software has enabled many amateur genealogists to plot the course of their family history. It seems that finding out who we are is an important modern concern.

When Alex Haley's epic story *Roots* was first produced as a mini-series in 1977, few expected it to generate such worldwide interest and acclaim. Based on Haley's family history, 'Roots' was watched by nineteen million viewers in the UK alone, and 160 million worldwide, which made it one of the most watched programmes in the history of broadcasting. According to the BBC website, only the final episode of 'M*A*S*H' and the legendary 'Dallas' episode 'Who shot J.R.?' eclipsed 'Roots' in the ratings war! Haley's story stretches back seven generations to a young tribesman in the Gambia called Kunta Kinte. From these African roots the family history unveils a story of human dignity that dared to battle with enslavement and pernicious cruelty. On an accompanying BBC blog-site many people voice their gratitude to this epoch-making series. For those who felt ostracized or even enslaved, connections were made and a common heritage explored. Various people claim that Haley's exploration into his family's past produced a sense of liberation and, to others, redemption.

But what of our roots of faith, of longing and belonging to God? When we give ourselves permission to venture into our past, known and unknown, we somehow touch upon the essence of our humanity, even if this is experienced through the lives of those who have gone before us. Jesus' roots have, for many biblical scholars, been a quest to discover a historical person. Certainly the quest has revealed marks of liberation and redemption. Jesus' lineage was through David, the hero of the Jewish faith, the shepherd boy turned warrior king. Jesus' arrival had been long awaited, announced and proclaimed through the centuries by the agents of God, the prophets. His ancestors of the faith had crossed many borders and fought various battles because God's heritage, the covenant promise, was worth preserving. The promise, however, was not easily recognized; it needed time to grow and flourish in order to satisfy fully the vocation that God intended. Today, the people of promise, those who carry the gift of faith, are presented with a challenge: how can this God-given heritage grow and develop in the lives of our children? How can we be true to our promise as parents? How can the covenant relationship that we establish with our children be fully realized? The promises which we make as adults, to care for and nurture our children, are vocational choices, laying down the foundation stones of welfare and community living.

The story of God's people, first through the Old and New Testaments and then through the lives of the Church Fathers, is characterized by the signs of the covenant relationship, sacrifice and trust. This relationship is the responsibility of the whole community of faith. The march to holiness is a calling from our birth to our death. Today the Church recognizes these formative stages of spiritual development through the ceremonies of baptism, confirmation and ordination, which define the pattern of vocation. The anointing and initiation rites are sacraments which formalize and legitimize passages of growth and development in a sacred soul. The sacraments are not permanent relics of an encounter in time, but are vehicles of growth past, present and future, into the love of God.

Welcoming the child

The east window of Monmouth School Chapel, where I am currently chaplain, is dedicated to the child, displaying biblical accounts of children who have been marked out and called by God. The window emphasizes the place of childhood within the scheme of God's kingdom. I like to imagine that the boys at school have each had opportunity to do some window-gazing themselves, that they might be distracted by these scenes, and imagine and question and wonder what part they might play in them. One of these stories paints the picture of the infant Jesus being presented in the temple in Jerusalem. For the old man Simeon, Jesus' arrival had been long awaited. The presentation of Jesus in the temple marked the contented conclusion of the life of Simeon, the priest:

> 'Master, now you are dismissing your servant in peace, according to your word; for my eyes have seen your salvation, which you have prepared in the presence of all peoples, a light for revelation to the Gentiles and for glory to your people Israel.'
>
> (Luke 2:29–32)

The response of Jesus' parents to these words was one of amazement (Luke 2:33). An old man saw in the infant child God's vocation, and his song echoes the voice of ages past for liberation, redemption and hope. Jesus was to deliver this hope to God's people. In the great paintings and stained-glass images of the presentation of Jesus, Simeon receives the child from his mother. It is as if this is a homecoming, an initiation which speaks of Jesus' belonging to the sacred space which is his Father's house. It is striking to reflect upon the dedication of those who have prayed for this homecoming. In the characters of Simeon and Anna, we have a priestly and prophetic representation of a nation's desire and longing, not just of their generation but throughout all generations.

The presentation of Jesus reveals something about the preparation that a community of faith invests into the welcome of children. This will be explored further in the chapter on baptism. The point here is that our roots, our heritage, who we are as people and where we call home, have much to do with preparation, of laying down the foundations for the welcome, support and nurture of children in our own faith communities. The widow Anna had invested a great deal: 'she never left the temple but worshipped there with fasting and prayer night and day' (Luke 2:37b). What might Anna's example say to us?

In laying down these foundations of covenant and community for our children, we understand that calling and vocation are not the exclusive possessions of the adult world but the timeless marks and signs of God's creative and redeeming purpose. In considering the gift of faith, where it comes from, and how it has been fashioned and changed by forces earthly and heavenly, a profound sense emerges that God is working through his people and with his creation to call us through frontiers, thresholds and borders to sacred places.

Crossing the border

Four years ago, I made the decision to leave parish life and, in doing so, opened myself up to an uncertain future. I crossed the border. In an instant my journey took me to a different country – my identity had changed. Travelling with my burgeoning family, I was to be marked by this new direction. I had come from an inner urban parish in West London. I had been priest of this parish for three short years which had been committed to health and healing, building bridges and restoring a sense of hope after the murder of my predecessor.[2] The decision to leave this place was taken with a great deal of soul searching. The reasons were various and complex, but it seemed that the foundation stones for this vocational change had been laid down for me.

Crossing the borderlands is a pilgrim's journey. By crossing the border I had made the passage from London to Monmouth, from

England to Wales. My vocational identity had also changed. I had made an ontological shift from parish priest to school chaplain. The impact of the move was particularly acute as it was marked by a time of bereavement for the parish that I left behind. Yet I had felt called to this new place. It was as though I had been disturbed and then pulled into a change of being. I was to be a school chaplain and teacher, unknown territory in what the Church defines as sector ministry. My uncertain hope was that the vocational shift into chaplaincy might prove to be holy ground. I was somehow familiar with the terrain of these borderlands. It was as if I had been here before. I felt a sense of homecoming, like a pilgrim. Perhaps this land had been a long-awaited destination, not of my own knowing, but God's.

The crossing of the borderland marked a new stage of journeying. In leaving parish life, I felt as though I had left my original map behind in which the distinctive landmarks of ministry as I knew it – the daily office, the liturgical rhythm of the week, the round of baptisms, weddings and funerals – were to be replaced by a new set of landmarks: timetables, the curriculum and the school bell. The transition period marked, therefore, a painful attempt to discover God in the less distinctive places in the belief that 'all of God [is] in every place' (Berryman, 2002a, p. 60). In fact, I had no choice. I adventured to the less revealed places of divine calling where the overt signs of Christian ministry were mostly absent. My vocation as father and husband was to lead to a deeper understanding of calling, perhaps not in its traditional sense but through the eyes of a borderman.

Cairn building

Many hill walkers share a common language when they describe aspects of the outdoor experience, the pleasures of trekking and the underlying dangers too. Without a map and compass, the hills can pose serious questions. Without a knowledge of the mountains, the landscape can claim lives. For this reason many hill walkers understand the significance of small heaps of stone and rock called cairns. These stones act as a navigational guide to any who have lost the path, protruding out of the horizon as mist or darkness descends. They have been slowly built up through years of diligent care by pilgrims for pilgrims. The cairns are also situated upon mountains and hill tops to mark the summit, the journey's peak.

In the Old Testament, Abram and Moses, the covenant builders, were also cairn builders. They created stone altars on the sacred places where they had experienced God (Genesis 12:7; 13:18; Exodus 17:15; 24:4). The stone altars literally marked out holiness for future pilgrims to encounter. These stone monuments represented the meeting place of human searching and God's interaction. Such places demonstrate the nature of vocation where the divine will is wondrously seen and felt.

The marks or signs of calling are analogous to the ceremonies of passage that the Christian Church calls the rites of anointing and initiation. Baptism, confirmation and ordination mark out an individual as sacred to God. Symbols are used within these sacramental occasions as signposts, or what St Augustine calls 'the outward signs' of transformation, of a changed state of being. The rites of anointing and initiation belong to the ministry of the frontier. The significance or purpose of these rites should never be underestimated. They are located at the very edge of the Church's life, at the transition point between the sacred and the secular. The markings of our discipleship, our journey into God and his creation, also reveal a holy tension. At one level, the rites of anointing and initiation deepen our membership of faith but, at another, they set up a challenge to see the world in a new light. This tension is rightly sponsored by the Church, receiving seekers who are not only marked by the boundary but who also become signs of the boundary.

Called home

The term Welsh Marches describes the mainly English counties which rub against the Welsh Border. The word 'marches' is derived from the Anglo-Saxon *mearc* or *mark* in Old English. Mark signified a 'boundary', and later 'the sign of a boundary'. A broader definition of the word also includes borders, frontiers and thresholds. In this way, the origin of the term 'marches' links to the wider theme of pilgrimage.

Why, though, did I feel this call so keenly towards the border country? Perhaps part of the answer was that this place felt familiar, known and real. A popular mantra for my journey has been and continues to be: 'Where is home?' This is a question which pushes us to the limits of our 'landscape of life'.[3] For me, home is a place of welcome and belonging, a place of purpose and fulfilment. I had somehow sensed that this small stretch of border country was home. Certainly the imagination has no small part to play here. Imagination is a great gift of faith, a divine gift. Yet, through prayer, instinct and imagining, I became aware of a pulling or a tugging towards this border country, this homeland.

After our arrival in Monmouth, we still sought definitive answers to the question of 'Where is home?' A new friend, experienced and wise, offered an explanation. She was quite matter-of-fact about why we had come here. She told us that this borderland had been the locus of community living for many generations. The stone and soil were saturated with prayer, worship and praise. It was the gift of these past generations that had marked out our passage. This is the way of vocation, the crossing of the borderlands through the gift of inherited faith.

The religious life, which has been so endemic in this part of the world, is not a forgotten memory but belongs to the 'landscape of memories'[4] where new life is harvested. Moreover, the religious communities that have made a home here have given a gift of faith which is very much a living entity – a sacred treasure. The history of prayer is long and rich: the Augustinians at Llanthony in the Black Mountains, the Cistercians at Tintern and Grace Dieu (near Monmouth), and the Benedictines in Chepstow, Abergavenny, Usk, Monmouth, Grosmont and Skenfrith, among others. These communities have marked out a way of life and a faith for future generations which is a great heritage. A calling is the realization that this heritage is a living gift of faith available for ourselves, our children and our children's children. It is this sense of hope that inspired the writing of this book: that the inheritance of faith is readily available for all to receive today. Our children, despite the obvious threats of this age, have an opportunity to develop and grow in faith, to answer the calling of God. Children are border people, the people of God, marked by holiness and standing in the borderlands of faith and truth and beauty.

Chapter 2

Legends

It takes just nine months for a child to be ready to come from the womb, but it took innumerable generations of prophets and scribes, mothers and fathers, poets and lawgivers, before the language of God's people was ready for the Word of love to be made flesh.

(Radcliffe, 2008, p. 40)

Ancient stories

Borderlands are steeped in legend. Once upon a time, when the lives of the saints and martyrs were first described, these legends probably had some basis in fact. It would seem, however, that our ancestors knew no bounds when it came to telling a good yarn. Indeed, so enthusiastic was their love of the saints and martyrs that in time the term *legend* 'came to signify the untrue, or rather an event based on tradition' (Brewer, 1988). Legends are, therefore, stories which have been passed down through the generations, which have been revised, adapted, embellished and enriched. Their propensity to be exaggerated and adorned is a mark of their appeal and significance; the stories are repeated because they are good stories. They are very frequently, though by no means definitively, stories with a moral undertone. Perhaps we can identify with them; perhaps there is something in them that speaks of where we are at; or perhaps they reflect our own journey, our own sense of where it is that we are travelling.

In twenty-first-century Britain, the word *legend* might seem somewhat remote. Yet ancient legends continue to have their place in contemporary culture. In Monmouth, the place of legend building has particular historical significance. Geoffrey of Monmouth, a monk whose life and work was imbedded in the Christian religious tradition, was thought to have lived in or around Monmouth in the 1100s. It was Geoffrey's classic book *The History of the Kings of Britain*[1] which placed Monmouth on the literary map forever. The book's value, past and present, cannot be overlooked. In twelfth-century Wales, it was second only to the Bible and, beyond its borders, the book was subsequently translated into a vast number of European languages.

A recent exhibition about Geoffrey in my local parish church of St Mary's posed a series of questions about this ancient figure. Was Geoffrey a storyteller or a historian? A chronicler of 'the truth', a romantic writer, a political propagandist, a spin-doctor or a liar?[2] However historians have responded to and debated these questions over the centuries, beyond dispute it seems is Geoffrey's lasting influence on stories as we know them today, most notably the legend of King Arthur. The legend of King Arthur is now some 1,500 years old. Through the centuries it has seen many an adaptation, initially, thanks to Geoffrey's legacy, in the form of medieval and epic romances, Shakespearian plays and, in more recent decades, in the form of novels, comic strips and various films. More recently of course, the internet has had its own hand in its survival. A quick surf on the web bears testimony to how King Arthur's life chronicles have literally been cut and pasted across sites, at times repeated word for word, at others altered here and there. This new kind of chronicling seriously lacks the narrative richness handed down to us by Geoffrey of Monmouth and the subsequent writers of the medieval histories and romances. All the same, even a replicated summary of King Arthur's life is a stark reminder of his legendary status. Attributed with leading the British defence against the Saxon invaders in the early sixth century, his legend is torn between history and fantasy, between brutal facts and fictional romance. It is of no surprise that he has persisted through the centuries, emerging as a versatile if elusive figure, whose very intangibility secures his place in the historical landscape that is our imagination.

In his book *Why Go To Church?* Timothy Radcliffe looks at how an individual's story can become located in a wider story. He draws on examples from contemporary writing as well as biblical testaments to illustrate this; most notably, the stories of Moses and Mary who, as a result of being called by God, were 'led ... to inhabit different stories', stories which related to their ancestors but which would also reshape future history (Radcliffe, 2008, p. 36). Mary's place in both ancestral and future stories underpins the Magnificat, her response to Gabriel's news that she is bearing God's Son:

> Surely, from now on all generations will call me blessed;
> for the Mighty One has done great things for me,
> and holy is his name ...
> He has helped his servant Israel,
> in remembrance of his mercy,
> according to the promise he made to our ancestors,
> to Abraham and to his descendants for ever.
>
> (Luke 1:48b–49, 54–55)

Mary's Song of Praise reveals how stories root the individual in both the old and new, past and future. Stories are not finite entities, the sole property of any one individual, but they cascade down through the generations, generating new meaning, new purpose, a new sense of 'who we think we are'.

Family legends

A theological approach to questions of 'Who do we think we are?' has something in common with a psychological and systemic approach to human stories. In systemic practice, which started out as family therapy, the problem is not seen as located in a particular individual but in the system of individuals of which the problem is a part. While the family, for example, might have a strong script about what the problem is or, more specifically, to whom the problem is attached, systemic practice seeks to broaden thinking beyond any one individual, and create an understanding of the difficulties that identifies patterns of communication and relationship as critical.[3] As part of this systemic process, the importance of storytelling and story-listening emerges:

> Everyone creates, tells, listens to, changes, and retells stories. As
> stories are told, people name and shape the meaning of the daily

events of their lives and communicate that meaning to others …
through familial and community stories, voices are shared and
joined. Stories allow for both continuity and change. Heritage is
passed on, even as new tellers and listeners reshape and call
forth different concerns, issues and details.

(Roberts, 1994, p. 1)

The role of storytelling, therefore, so implicit in our everyday, is not
to be underestimated. It can help define who we are and where we
are going, it has the power to shape not only our lives but also the
lives of others. The stories we tell our children and the stories they
tell us are constantly changing and adapting according to the rubric
of our days and our different life stages. Some stories will be passed
over and quickly forgotten; others will be chewed on and debated,
persisting perhaps into the annals of family history, perhaps for as
long as our children will remember, perhaps for longer.

In his paper, 'Scripts and Legends in Families and Family
Therapy', John Byng Hall calls these latter stories – those stories,
that is, that persist over generations – 'family legends':

Family legends have a particular place in family mythology.
There are those coloured and colourful stories that are told time
and time again – in contrast to other information about the
family's past, which fades away. Although they are ostensibly told
because they are interesting, the way they are told frequently
indicates how the family *should* behave – a form of moral tale.

(Byng Hall, 1988, p. 169)

Byng Hall goes on to tell a legend which has been in his family some
222 years. Having told the story, he considers what its key theme
is and then explores how this theme has impacted on the pattern of
his own life. In the last instance, he sets about unearthing the story's
'moral'. To his surprise and fascination, he discovers that the story,
despite its age, goes way beyond achieving anecdotal status, and in
fact has a powerful resonance with the patterns and themes of his
own life. Byng Hall's discovery has always intrigued me. For that
reason I have decided to set myself a similar task: namely, to embark
on my own journey of family legends. My own story is not half so

old, but nonetheless it is legendary to me. It is the story of my grand-parents and, to my mind, has two main strands. But I shall try not to jump ahead of myself, and simply tell it.

The story of Nicholas

My grandmother's first child was called Nicholas. His photo stood beside the clock on the mantelpiece: soft featured, about three years old, his place in our family was constant. As a small child, I would frequently ask my grandmother about Nicholas. It was a kind of ritual, I suppose. She would regale me with anecdotes I knew almost by heart and I would listen. As the years passed, however, and we entertained other rituals, I forgot the stories that had enter-tained me so often when I was young.

When my grandmother died in my early twenties, I berated myself that I had never written the stories down. But what, in truth, might I have written? The quality of my grandmother's narration? Her laughter, perhaps, as she remembered? The tears that, for those sweet hours, spoke only of joy? Or the singular realization that dawned on me one day, perhaps when I was nine or ten, that Nicholas did not simply belong to a photograph and stories past. He had lived and played too once, just like me, and that same boy, my mother's brother, my grandparents' firstborn, they were one and the same, and somehow I had not made the connection.

When the connection was finally made, I said nothing. I remember my grandmother's face. Nothing changed; it did not need to. She had long since carried this grief and no small realization on my part would disturb that. But when next I visited my grand-mother, or perhaps the time after, I no longer asked her about the child whose short life had until then captivated me. I did not ask and my grandmother did not offer. It was not consciously done on either part, but the carefree revelations of our discourse ended when I first understood that Nicholas had died. And when, a gener-ation later, my grandmother also died, her grief for her son became part of my own grief: a sadness and regret that I had left those stories, treasured and timeless, buried in childhood.

Nicholas died during the Second World War. My grandfather was away in India and not allowed home on leave. As the end of the war approached, my mother's curiosity about what her father might look like intensified. When he did return, he did not exactly conform to her expectations. Tall for his generation, he had lost several stone overseas, having contracted an illness which was for the next five years to play Russian roulette with his life. In time, it seemed clear to everyone that he was dying. Given days to live by the medical profession, he had a chance reunion with an old family friend who had been a surgeon in India during the war and said he had seen something similar. It was a long shot but the cure, as he knew it, was to flood my grandfather's body with arsenic. They had nothing to lose. My mother was prepared to expect her father to die during the night. In the event, contrary to all predictions, my grandfather survived; and somewhere in a textbook in a place I do not know it is apparently written down that my grandfather was the first man in Europe to be cured from the said tropical disease by arsenic flooding.

I think I would want to make that textbook the starting point for my very own, 'Who do you think you are?' I would want to pull the book down from some dusty archive, turn its leaves with my own hand and read with my own eye the bare facts which have, for as far back as I can remember, rooted themselves in family folklore. Fact, myth or legend? I strongly believe the first but would, I suppose, have to prepare myself to be disappointed just in case. I would not want to be disappointed. I would not want to rewrite family history with some drab, second-place account of my grandfather's recovery. But, fact or fiction, the legend is, for me at least, quite safe. It is these legends which help shape us and feed us, which lend a hand in our identity, formation and even vocation. Setting myself, therefore, that same task which Byng Hall set for himself – 'to discern the moral behind the legend' – I am starting to understand that in my grandfather's legend lay a very distinct 'moral': a profound message handed down to his children and children's children about the sacredness of life; an understanding, however unconscious, that life can never truly be valued if we do not keep in mind the fragile beauty of that sacred thread which binds our life to this world and carries us to the next.

'A happy death'

My grandfather, larger than life with stories to match, always maintained that a man could decide when he was ready to die. I never really knew what he meant until he reached his own old age and my grandmother died before him. From that day on, while he continued to value life as sacred, I watched him set about dying with the same faith, courage and determination that I had witnessed in him so many times before. As I watched him and, with many others, accompanied him on his particular journey, I started to understand that his own battle with illness and near encounter with death as a young man had given him a preparedness for dying which, utterly unequipped as I am to articulate myself, is what Christopher Jamison calls 'a happy death'. Jamison writes:

> Clearly, dying at an advanced age, knowing that we are dying, surrounded by the loving support of friends and family, are elements of a happy death. But a happy death can take many forms. As part of our journey to find happiness, if we can appreciate what happiness means in the context of death, which, after all, is the one future experience we will all share, then we may have found an understanding of happiness that will also serve us well in life.
>
> (Jamison, 2008, p. 25)

For my grandfather, though he, unlike so many of his peers before him, had the privilege and blessing of dying surrounded by family and loved ones – though he faced death head on and spoke throughout of his 'childlike' faith, his great sense of a path ahead – there was nothing easy about his preparation for dying. It was, I now realize, only during the last days of his life that he started to place his own son's death in its wider context – in the context, that is, of the Second World War, a war in which people died in multitudes, and in which people time and again were denied the possibility of burying their loved ones; of simply saying goodbye to those they cherished most.

Alongside my grandfather's courage and determination – his deep-rooted faith and sense of purpose which journeyed with him in the last weeks of his life – he was also greatly troubled by a particular image which would not leave him. The image was one of mass graves, of digging and of burying countless men in the desert. He spoke of it repeatedly, deeply disturbed by what he saw. In the end my mother asked his parish priest to visit him. The priest came and spoke to him about events in his life which had, as far as I knew, been buried themselves until then. Together the priest and my grandfather made the connection that, at a time when my grandfather was digging the graves for his fellow men, his own son had been dying – his firstborn from whom he was given no leave-taking, whom he was not allowed to come home and bury.

Internal borderlands

When I look back now as an adult at the figure of Nicholas, I can only speculate at the role he has had in my life. One generation removed, his impact can be nothing but indirect. I did not know him, lose him, grieve for him. And yet, along with my mother, my grandparents, my extended family, I have always felt that I knew him. As a young child, the boundaries of this knowledge were crossed tirelessly and without effort as I joined my grandmother in the stories of her firstborn and, in doing so, was given an insight into her identity, her formation and her vocation as mother. At the time I did not know this, of course. I have never, until now, given it conscious thought. The individual stories themselves have long since faded and form only impressions on my mind. All the same, as I write, I start to sense that Nicholas's story has, for the duration of my mother's childhood, for the duration of my own childhood, and perhaps, I cannot tell, for the duration of generations to come, been handed down for safe-keeping. We have, both consciously and unconsciously, been asked to keep it, to remember it, never to forget. And in that process of not forgetting, I find I start to understand something of the infinite capacity of my grandparents' love, of their courage and survival, their overwhelming ability to hold in mind – the same ability which remembered me throughout my own childhood and early adulthood; which handed down an untold gift I hope to give my children; one which comes with a cost but which is priceless, which sets itself no bounds, but which tries us, tests us, and demands that we cross our own internal borderlands.

When I returned to work after my first child was born, my trainee at the time asked, was there anything I would do differently now that I was a mother myself? With the sum total of eight months' experience behind me, my reply was both instinctive and unguarded: that while I did not know if there was anything I would *do* differently as such, I was now starting to understand how parenthood could take one to the very edge of one's feelings. I remember she seemed quite shocked. A confession of my own fallibility was clearly not what she had been expecting. Nor, I confess, was it what I had been expecting. In those months of preparation for our first child's birth, in those long, still hours I had spent imagining how he would be, how he would grow, I did not really stop to think how parenthood would change me, how it would interlock and grapple with my own sense of identity, my own formation, my own understanding of calling or vocation.

In his book *Lost Icons,* Rowan Williams articulates the need for adults to develop and change if they are to care for and nurture children:

> The 'safest' adult to have around is one who is aware of having *grown* – one, that is, who knows in his or her own experience how transitions are made from one sort of choosing to another (which also means one who hasn't forgotten what it is *like* to be a child).
> (Williams, 2007, p. 35)

For my own part, I am, I think, aware in recent years of having *grown*, but aware also more compellingly yet of how fragile my own growth is, sliding as it does between states of self-knowledge and ignorance, between self-sacrifice and utter selfishness. It will take more than time and experience to reconcile these states – a life's pilgrimage, I am starting to discover. In choosing to be a mother, I unwittingly made a choice to cross my own internal borderlands; to encounter not once but again and again, year in, year out, the stories, old and new, legendary or true, not only of my relationship to others but of my potential, however fragile, for relationship with God.

Integrating Mind and Spirit (Part 1)

Who Do We Think We Are?

When we seek to foster our children's identity, we need to understand our own: that is, our own longing and belonging to God. In exploring our personal roots, we begin to understand who we are in relation to others. We see ourselves in a wider context which includes our geography, our family, our personal beliefs or faith, our community and our culture; in other words, our heritage. From a faith perspective, we understand that our individual story is marked, not only by time and place but by the manifestation of the divine. Our story becomes God's story and God's story becomes our story. From a psychological perspective, our individual stories can be placed in the wider system of family relationships. We start to understand how family stories across generations have helped shape who we are today.

This renewed understanding of who we are is not confined to an historic search. As curiosity about ourselves and our heritage deepens, the more alive we become to a living, breathing faith which spans time, past, present and future. When we understand our individual stories in this broader context, we deepen our awareness not only of ourselves but of others, and ultimately of our relationship to God. The desire to understand who we are is, therefore, one which extends and pushes both our spiritual and emotional boundaries. This desire is the source of our calling. It transforms the individual to sharing the gift of a faith journey which somehow reorders and repatriates individual lives into a family structure, that of the Church.

Called to respond

As adults, we have a responsibility to provide our children with a sense of their heritage, both in terms of faith and family. When we hear Mary's Song of Praise, we are reminded that God calls his children throughout all generations. In reflecting upon the following passage, how might you respond personally or corporately (for example, as a family, school or church) to its calling?

The Magnificat

My soul magnifies the Lord,
  and my spirit rejoices in God my Saviour,
for he has looked with favour on the lowliness of his servant.
  Surely, from now on all generations will call me blessed;
for the Mighty One has done great things for me,
  and holy is his name.
His mercy is for those who fear him
  from generation to generation.
He has shown strength with his arm;
  he has scattered the proud in the thoughts of their hearts.
He has brought down the powerful from their thrones,
  and lifted up the lowly;
he has filled the hungry with good things,
  and sent the rich away empty.
He has helped his servant Israel,
  in remembrance of his mercy,
according to the promise he made to our ancestors,
  to Abraham and to his descendants for ever.

Part 2

Identity

Footsteps

Footsteps follow us.
If we could count them we would
Know the number of the stars
And grains of desert sand.
They are shod for strength
But our shoes stumble a little
Searching the path.

We are taking the way
To God's house bearing
Our gift to his table. We hold
The child close in our arms for
He has travelled oceans to find us.

On our palms is a map printing
The signposts, mist swirling
On flesh, dampening our faces.
A voice says come bring the child
And multitudes sigh swelling in
Whispers we are here, all here,
They reply.

The child stirs as light
Paints the west window.
I name you, washing you with
Waters of baptism.
We name you, calling you into
The congregation of Christ's family,
God names you, signing you with
The touch of his love.

Sacred vessel can you trust us
To travel this map, help discover
Each marking? Who will follow,
Who lead as years grow new
Cairns of our struggles, our partings?
Look the candle is lit, the procession
Is starting; come let us tread in those
Footsteps that hollowed the sand
At our birthing.

Dallin Vines

Chapter 3

Baptism

The waters of baptism pour out from their desert source. The waters of the Jordan flow like sacramental channels providing new life for God's people. These same waters initiated the baptism of Jesus. The Gospels reveal that God identified his pleasure in his Son as he emerged out of the Jordan River: so too God identifies his pleasure in all who are baptized. Identity, the naming of the one before God, is central to our understanding not only of baptism but of childhood also. Before God can invite his creation into a purposeful relationship, the creation is given a divine identity: 'Then God said, "Let us make humankind in our image, according to our likeness"' (Genesis 1: 26a). The initiation of baptism means that God calls the child by name for the first time, the Spirit of God descends on the child in fulfilment of God's promise to all his people of the covenant. God names the child, bestows upon it a divine identity, and celebrates the crossing of the borderland. In this chapter I will consider how the rite of baptism can help us discover the integrity of children in God's divine plan. Baptism is used as a metaphor for the welfare of, and responsibility for, the child in God's kingdom.

Baptism is the initiation rite which signs or marks the individual with the motif of death and life, the cross, the ultimate marks of identification of the Christian pilgrimage. Translated from the Greek, baptism refers to a ritual washing; meaning 'to dip, plunge or submerse', it requires the drowning or the dying of the individual to the calling of the world (Colossians 3:1–4, Ephesians 2:5). The baptized is reborn out of these waters and called into a new relationship with God and God's world, and that relationship is an invitation of discovery. The challenge that such an invitation presents concerns our own knowledge of identity, of real self-knowing. As Thomas Merton states, 'The secret of my identity is hidden in the love and mercy of God' (1949, p.19). If we are not fully open to discover who we are, we are unlikely to recognize the invitation that is given to us as a gift. This, then, is the landscape of discovery which is much travelled by Christian pilgrims.

The Big Idea

In the summer of 2008, I organized a pilgrimage for the boys of Monmouth School. The project was called the Big Idea and it entailed a two-day walk along the Offa's Dyke path from Monmouth School Chapel to Llanthony Abbey in the Black Mountains. My hope, the Big Idea, was that the boys would engage with the world around them; that the experience of beauty in the revelation of nature might elicit a connection between creation and our place within it; that the rhythm of walking and talking might nurture what Thomas Merton called the 'seeds of contemplation' within them:

> Therefore each particular being, in its individuality, its concrete nature and entity, with all its own characteristics and its private qualities and its own inviolable identity, gives glory to God by being precisely what he wants it to be here and now, in the circumstances ordained for it by His Love and His infinite Art.
>
> (Merton, 1949, p. 15)

We were to follow the footsteps of our patron of Wales, St David, Dewi Sant, who was believed to have had a monastic cell at Llanthony. The boys all received a pilgrim's manual which contained maps, short liturgies for the beginning and end of the pilgrimage, as well as cross-curricular information sheets supplied by many of the school's departments. The boys carried only the bare minimum – the manual and food and water (and a rugby ball). All of the overnight equipment had been transported to the farm where we were to pitch our tents alongside a midsummer's fair. The pilgrims were of mixed ages with mixed motivations. Many decided that the Big Idea would be a good excuse to miss Saturday school. Some wanted to prove to themselves capable of achieving the 30-mile walk in two days, while others held a quiet, noble intention that they would learn something new about themselves and others around them. We were sent on our way by a short liturgy introducing the purpose of pilgrimage and holy journeying:

> Pilgrimage is traditionally a journey to a holy place – a place where saints have walked, a place where God has met people and blessed them. People through the ages have journeyed with God on pilgrimage – to perform a penance to ask for healing ... Pilgrimage is an opportunity to travel lightly, to walk free of daily routines, to meet people, to make friends, to enjoy and celebrate God's creation. An opportunity, too, in the travelling, the conversations and the silences to reflect on the journey of our lives and on our journey homewards to God.
>
> (Paynter, 2002)

The boys were divided into groups, the older ones responsible for their younger charges. Familial patterns emerged and group identities were quickly established. By the end of the first day's walk, as we approached the border stronghold of White Castle, the nature of the pilgrimage had been shaped. That evening we all enjoyed the benefits of the Midsummer Fair including an historic re-enactment of the story of the blind man of White Castle, a hog roast and an obligatory campsite fire.

The following morning, we awoke to the sound of singing from one particular tent. The boys had been awoken to the idea of pilgrimage, albeit at 5 am. At breakfast, a tangible sense of excitement ran through the camp. New friends were arriving today to complete the pilgrimage. The sun had reappeared; we were carefree on this Sabbath day. The latter stage of our journey took us north-east of Abergavenny. The forty pilgrims (students and staff), who were aged between twelve and sixty-three, started their ascent onto a ridge which would eventually lead us to our destination. Conversations were in full flow and expectations high. The ruins of Llanthony were soon to be revealed, partially hidden below us in the shadow of the Ewyas Valley.

Our ridge walk exposed the pilgrims to the midsummer sun and driving wind. It was in the intensity of this light and sound that we surveyed the border landscape. The terrain revealed clear marks delineating Wales from England: the sedate and agricultural Welsh Marches to the right – that of English Herefordshire – and the bulk and brooding menace of the Black Mountains to the left, the ownership of Wales. We climbed down from the ridge to congregate once more in the church of St David, within the Abbey walls. We had claimed a place with at least one saint, Dewi Sant. By the end of the pilgrimage we had discovered more about ourselves and our landscape. The picture that I now frame in my mind's eye is one which for me describes borderland: the signs, marks and physical characteristics of people and culture, of lives and land. Not only is this image one that remains as a memory of the Big Idea pilgrimage, it is also a graphic metaphor for the search and meaning of identity, the search for our own sacred selves. The search, the calling, the pilgrimage is, I suggest, the embodiment of our baptism.

A *metanoia* calling

The Christian identity is bound up by a myriad of social, emotional and psychological pressures. Throughout late modernity and postmodernity, the therapeutic disciplines of psychology, psychiatry and psychotherapy have been guides, orienting the disoriented, bringing comfort and support to many lost souls. Yet a challenge exists for the individual in our contemporary 'I' culture for a balance to be struck between self-awareness and self-absorption. An imbalance of identity is displayed not just on an adult stage but permeates through to all ages, producing obstacles which potentially thwart the welfare of our children. If we continue to turn down the invitation to know God and thus know who we truly are, our self-knowledge will be undermined by the false gods of our age. So the main cause of this identity crisis is a movement away from the God who treasures our identity, who bids us to journey home to receive it. The action of turning around, of allowing God's grace to do its work is the *metanoia* that lies at the heart of Jesus' teaching: 'Repent, for the kingdom of heaven has come near' (Matthew 4:17). Repentance is the call to journey from the selfishness of individualism to an acceptance of our shared identity in the love of God.

Contemporary culture is in danger of transposing its own identity crisis upon childhood, branding children with the marks of self-absorption and individualism before all else. In contrast to this, baptism reflects God's image outwards to the world through the baptized. Rather than being shackled by the strictures of the adult world, God invites the child to grow freely.

The quest to discover one's self-identity would have been anathema to Jesus' followers. Individual identities in the first century were only obtained through relationship with others, through peers or family groups. This was an 'other-oriented' society in which people depended on others to provide them with a sense of meaning, of who they were.[1] Only God was designated with the title 'I AM', only God was worthy of personal self-identification. 'I AM WHO I AM,' proclaimed God to a questioning and rather hesitant Moses (Exodus 3:14). Indeed the Hebrew name for God, Yahweh, comes from the verb which means 'to exist, or to be'. The phrase in Greek, *Εγω ειμι*, or I AM, is given great emphasis in John's Gospel,[2] identifying Jesus to God the Father.

Today, where individualism is rife, Jesus' 'I am' sayings may well have lost their intended impact, for this is God the Father describing his relationship with his creation, and God the Son identifying himself with his Father's creation, echoing the proclamation of God at the beginning of his children's struggle for liberation. So when the Gospel writers describe Jesus deliberately placing a child – by definition, a person without rank or status – in front of him, and before his followers, an essential truth is dramatically choreographed. Age, status or hierarchy has no place in Jesus' mission. 'Truly I tell you, unless you change and become like children, you will never enter the kingdom of heaven' (Matthew 18:3). Today, the child before Jesus demonstrates how the loss of the 'other-oriented' identity has corroded our sense of God. The child helps us to rediscover our identity before God, our place in the human landscape: 'Human beings actually don't live "nowhere in particular" they live "somewhere", they have a landscape, a landscape literally of what's around them physically, and the landscape provided by the people who have made them who they are.'[3] Jesus' followers were being asked to cross the borderlands, to see the world and each other within a new landscape, understanding that God honours childhood, and the humility of the child, deeply. 'Whoever welcomes one such child in my name, welcomes me' (Matthew 18:5).

Jesus and the child become a sign of God's kingdom, participating in the nature of the relationship between the Father and the Son. Jesus enters the presence of the child as the child enters the presence of Jesus, mirroring the symbiotic nature of the Father and the Son. The child is obedient to Jesus as the Son is to the Father, obedient but not subjugated. Everything that Jesus chooses to do is as a result of his divine calling to God's authority.[4] The child is free to choose also, to determine his own future, although the irresistible presence of God, the kingdom's calling, is ever near.

It is through the initiation of the child that we discover the paradigm for kingdom building. Far from seeking to place children in a place of prominence before others, Jesus enables his confused followers to understand who they are through the innocence of the child. Earlier in Jesus' ministry, John the Baptist also reverses the established roles and allows others to understand who they are through the innocence of Jesus. It is he who identifies Jesus through the Messianic designation, 'Lamb of God'.[5] Jesus, the innocent lamb, was seen to be of God and many were attracted to his divine persona. So the first grown-up encounter of the cousins, Jesus and John, was immersed not in water but in identity. By recognizing Jesus as the lamb, John recognized who he was called to be: 'Our discovery of God is, in a way, God's discovery of us' (Merton, 1949, p. 22). John ushers a statement of divine profundity: 'Here is the Lamb of God who takes away the sin of the world!' John is able to capture the nature of God's salvation plan in just a few words. He has not only identified who this newcomer is to his own disciples, he has also offered a summary of the purpose of Jesus' ministry to come.

John had made a name for himself as a desert wanderer through his ascetic looks and strange proclamations. He was marking out a way in the desert as his predecessor Isaiah had prophesied. John had a *metanoia* calling which was uncompromising and ultimately real enough to attract crowds of enquirers. John preached repentance of sin in order to establish a new life for the spirit. The spirit of God was made manifest to all who welcomed it; lives were converted to a new direction, a new way of being, and the agent of this change was baptism.

Endangering God's image

From a theological perspective, it can be argued that contemporary childhood is lacking real identity and purpose; that the child is being raised in a dangerously arid state where the third element of its formation, the spirit, is being seriously compromised. The needs and requirements of a fulfilling childhood are being isolated in a culture of consumerism where possession, desire and choice are the ethical standard. We may well recognize the current predicament:

> Our culture is confused about children. Concern for the rights of the child and for the protection of children from abuse is intense. Yet we continue to exploit them mercilessly. Children are ever more relentlessly exposed to commercial, social, educational pressures. They are helpless victims of our sinful structures.[6]

The essence of childhood is often misappropriated, in particular when the image of God is mistaken and abused. In our competitive age, we seem to be hell-bent on speeding through innocence. Childhood is at risk of being stolen by the presence of modern technology – the internet, mobile phones and computer gaming saturate recreational opportunities. The gifts of wonder, imagination and curiosity, which are the possession of the child-like, are becoming superfluous to our formation. The focus of our child enquiry seems, therefore, markedly counter-cultural and suggests that the source of divinity, which is innate in all infants, should be treasured and nurtured. The task of the Church is to kindle this flame and not allow it to be extinguished. Irenaeus of Lyons[7] (second century AD), one of the Apostolic Fathers, considered life to be a process of development, growing into the likeness of God. We might consider that childhood is but one stage towards this maturation. Born in the image of God as we are, our whole lives are a calling towards God's likeness. We endanger God's image when we lose sight of our own humanity. Losing sight of who we are as adults has particular consequences for childhood. This is the most critical stage of our human development – children's early experiences affect their lives as adults. The welfare of our young depends on allowing children to be children, in order that mind and spirit develop naturally, not encumbered by the 'sinful structures' of our time. John the Baptist reveals this common error to his desert audience.

John was living out his vocation in the desert, an unlikely location for a spiritual revival. He had heard the prayers of his forefathers in faith such as Isaiah and Malachi,[8] and was alive to the roots of his prophetic ancestry. So what might John the Baptist represent in terms of the identity of the child in the community of faith? In John's Gospel, in the passage preceding the baptism of Jesus, John the Baptist is interrogated by the Temple's holy men. The substance of their interrogation involves the matter of John's identity, his role and his vocation:

> This is the testimony given by John when the Jews sent priests and Levites from Jerusalem to ask him, 'Who are you?' He confessed and did not deny it, but confessed, 'I am not the Messiah.' And they asked him, 'What then? Are you Elijah?' He said, 'I am not.' 'Are you the prophet?' He answered, 'No.' Then they said to him, 'Who are you? Let us have an answer for those who sent us. What do you say about yourself?' He said,
> 'I am the voice of one crying out in the wilderness,
> "Make straight the way of the Lord"',
> as the prophet Isaiah said.
>
> (John 1:19–23)

John is clear about his human task as well as his divine responsibility. He is the forerunner. John's adult voice is clear, his vision is focused upon God's image. John is the representative of the welfare of Israel, the children of God. He is the one who provides the firm foundation for the development of faith. The interrogators cannot discern God's image in John, they cannot perceive his role. They try desperately to make John admit to being someone or something that he is not. The interrogators misappropriate his heritage, his faith and his calling. This same battle continues today in church and society where the forerunners of faith struggle to be the firm foundation of our children's journey into God's image.

Keepers of the promise

John the Baptizer has a specific mission, to prepare the way. The baptismal rite echoes John's task through the role of parents and godparents of infants and children. In the selection of godparents, particular adults are literally chosen to prepare the way for the child. As the child is presented to the Church community at the start of the baptismal service, the godparents are asked to make promises to the child and the Church that they will carry out their duty. 'Will you pray for them, draw them by your example into the community of faith and walk with them in the way of Christ?' (Common Worship).[9] These promises resonate with John's life work and that of the prophets before him and the apostles after him, praying for God's salvation to be realized, drawing people together to the source of that salvation, and preparing them to follow in the way. This is no small task for parents and godparents, an unachievable one if attempted without God's strength and grace.

The baptismal rite centres, however, upon the importance of promise, the loving and conscious decision to promote and enable faith to seed and flourish. A godparent's responsibility speaks powerfully about a child's well-being because it is here that a commitment is made through the relationship of godparent and godchild which is covenantal, bound by trust and hope. In God's covenantal relationship with his people, mutual responsibility rests upon the tenets of trust and hope. 'I will establish my covenant between me and you, and your offspring after you throughout their generations, for an everlasting covenant, to be God to you and to your offspring after you' (Genesis 17:7). The keepers of the promise have an apostolic duty not only to keep the faith, but to engage with it and enable it to grow. In order to live this covenantal relationship, the godparents are asked to become bearers of a sacred trust.[10] I will never fully know to what extent the prayers of my godparents, their interest and love, have played a part in my vocational journey; nor indeed how my own prayers for my godchildren will influence their journeys. However, the bond of trust and hope remains; God's grace does not diminish; my guardianship continues.

From a parent's point of view, I find myself in a constant tension between the practical and the possible. For example, I have every hope and intention of raising my children to 'walk by the light of faith' (CW),[11] but the reality of keeping the baptismal promises is a constant challenge. There is also a danger that we as adult Christians mirror much of the anxiety and unhappiness of the world rather than giving sufficient spiritual direction to our children. What might the liturgy of baptism say about parenting and caring for children in general? More explicitly, what might this initiation rite say about our Christian heritage and the gift of faith? The Christian tradition attempts to give direction. The rites of initiation are sacramental pathways, grounding the knowledge of our limited self-awareness, offering signs and symbols which keep us on the pilgrim route and lead us towards our homecoming.

Bad parenting

When I became a newly ordained deacon in the Church, baptism was one of my first official sacramental tasks. In the church where I was curate, the community was large and vibrant; many of the laity were trained and ready for action. Our baptismal policy had been developed over many years; it was commonsensical without being far-reaching. The lay members of the baptism team were given the contact details of those who had made an enquiry about baptism. These enquirers would normally be those living within the parish boundary with little or no contact with the church community. Members of the baptism team would visit the family and describe something of the meaning of baptism (its theology), and something about what to expect in the service (its liturgy). The pastoral visitor would then try to be present at the baptism service to support the family and be a possible source of friendship for the future. The services were scheduled for 3 pm on a Sunday afternoon so as to finish in time for the preparation of choral evensong. Potentially four infants were permitted to be baptized during these occasions and, with the full complement of family and friends, the church was filled with enquiry. Nearly all the infant baptisms were conducted in this way in accordance with the wishes of the family. Adult baptisms were normally conducted within a confirmation service while those children born within the church family were baptized in the context of the Sunday Eucharist. This type of baptismal pattern is fairly common among many of our larger parish churches throughout the land. Such a policy has logistical advantages but, inevitably, theological weaknesses.

The illustration is relevant to adults concerned for the welfare of the child as it demonstrates the church's vulnerability in its own role as parent. If we believe that baptism is the primary rite of initiation into the community of faith (past, present and future), it follows that the church family should be present. Being present is not about the civil niceties of being seen to care, but about the spiritual integrity of the whole church, about renewing our own baptismal vows, of sensing divine activity in the giving and receiving of a gift. Indeed, this is our corporate responsibility; in more general terms, to be present to all of our children in Church and in society. Baptism is the mark of faith not only upon the individual but upon the whole of Christ's Church. It should therefore follow that baptism is celebrated publicly with the whole church in participation. The holy water, the living spring, should touch all those assembled as a reminder of our identity in God, an identity which is still being shaped and formed.

The Church has, through the rite of baptism, a reciprocal responsibility to carry out its mission to the world. It is an imperative of the Gospel (Mark 10:13–14) not only to welcome children, or the community of the child – parents, godparents, family and friends – but also to grow as a result of this welcome. 'Baptism is not a spectator sport' (Myers, 2000, p. 22). The 'Big Idea' of baptism is for others to join our pilgrimage, our journey of faith without discriminating by age or fitness. The liturgy of baptism marks out the importance of being included into a community of faith, not just by one member of the baptism team, but by the whole family of the church.

Called to God

When recruiting for confirmation classes in my role as school chaplain, I am sometimes asked by parents whether, since their child has been christened, might this mean he has been baptized? I normally attempt a quick theological response along the lines of, 'Yes, they are one of the same thing. To be christened is to be likened to Christ, to be made one with him. It is about being members of the same community of faith, the Church.' Some are surprised by this; others relieved that their child has 'been done' after all! And so it was with the calling of Jesus' followers that, through praying and teaching and living the common life, his disciples became at one with him 'in thought, word and deed' (CW).[12] Our fellowship in Christ can never remain still. It urges us to move closer to God, to become like Christ. Indeed this seems to be the pattern that was born out by those first called by Jesus. We do not have much information regarding their baptism but we do know that they were baptized (John 4:2, Acts 2:38, etc.) in order that their gift, their apostolic witness, be given to others. The picture of life in the new covenant painted here conveys a sense of dynamism where the excitement of the faith extended not only into new neighbourhoods but also into new generations. Baptism was given generously. In the same spirit today, baptism is given generously so that it may become the calling of all, starting from the moment a child is born. Children are, therefore, integral to this witness. The sacrament of baptism is a powerful sign of commitment and unity. God's covenant is for his new creation to become like Christ.

For those early followers, the process of being christened, of being likened to God, was life-changing. The impact of their transition from old to new, from nameless to named, from lost to found, produced, however, more questions than answers. The disciple Peter demonstrates something of our own anxiety when we approach the borderland, the threshold of a new life in Christ. Jesus and his disciples were in the region known as Caesarea Philippi. Caesarea was the new city built by Herod the Great and named after the Roman emperor's son. The Roman occupying forces believed Caesar to be a god. Jesus asks the ultimate question to his disciples in a place built as a tribute to a god of human making, 'Who do you say that I am?' The question was asked within a specific context, for Jesus was travelling to Jerusalem, a city built to the glory of God, his Father. It was Peter who first cried out the answer to Jesus' question, like an impetuous student determined to impress his teacher. Peter was chosen by Christ to be the rock upon which the Church would stand. He was given this duty because he was the one who acknowledged Jesus to be the Christ, the anointed one, the Messiah, the Son of the living God. So Peter is awarded the title of Cephas, the rock. He is given to us as a hero of our faith, not because he is pious or saintly, but because he displays the fullness of his own humanity and, therefore, God's likeness. 'Who am I for you?' we are asked as we cross the frontier, a question which continues to be heard as we struggle onwards.

Peter only mentions baptism once in his pastoral letters but, when he does, conveys a sense of Easter promise, the hope of salvation:

> And baptism, which this prefigured, now saves you – not as a removal of dirt from the body, but as an appeal to God for a good conscience, through the resurrection of Jesus Christ, who has gone into heaven and is at the right hand of God, with angels, authorities, and powers made subject to him.
>
> (1 Peter 3:21–22)

It is this promise of Easter which today's adults, the carers, the parents, teachers and priests are asked to hand on as the heritage of faith. Perhaps a renewal of hearts and minds is necessary as we consider the welfare of our children. If we are to work with Christ in the nurture of 'a holy nation' the support of the youngest members of our community is key. The responsibility of the Church, the christened, the priesthood of all believers, is to renew the possibility of faith for others. As members of the community of faith, it is our duty and our joy, alongside Peter, to respond to Jesus' question, 'But you, who do you say that I am?' (Matthew 16:15) with a loud, unequivocal, corporate voice: 'You are the Christ!' In recognizing the Christ, we understand the significance of our own calling which involves the whole community of faith, of all ages.

The school of baptism

If we are called by God to discover who we are through the life of the Church, the body of Christ, the tradition of the 'called people' becomes a sign for the Church today. In a most profound sense, God is crossing the borderlands of childhood with us. It is a child who is worshipped, who is called by God, who is the light of the world. Jesus, the child, is our paradigm for discovery. When Jesus was presented to the priest Simeon soon after his birth, God appeared in a new light, in human form, vulnerable and weak. Such are the occasions throughout our calling when we witness epiphanies not only in one another but in our children, seeing the world in a new light as we seek to imitate the life of Christ through baptism:

> See? The light is still spreading out. It is filling up the room. Just because you can't see it anymore doesn't mean that it is gone. Anywhere you go in the room today, there it will be. Our room will be full of invisible light. Your light. The light you received on the day of your baptism or the light you will receive.
>
> (Berryman, 2002b, p. 76)

The baptism candidates (or catechumens, as they were known in the early Church) were traditionally schooled to understand the doctrines of belief, the nature of the liturgy and the Church. Their graduation took place during the Easter vigil on the night of Holy Saturday after undergoing the necessary time of penitence that is Lent. The catechumens were received into the arms of Mother Church as the community of faith celebrated the story of salvation. The two worlds of death and life, of darkness and light co-exist both in the ritual of the three holy days, the triduum preceding Easter, as well as in the rite of baptism. The catechumens participating in the paschal liturgy would have been in no doubt that the light of the world prevails. God wins a costly victory over death and the gift of this victory is presented to the baptized as the gift of freedom.

The gift of baptism presents so many layers of meaning that its meaning is, on occasion, difficult to grasp. As parish priest, I visited many families who were enquiring about the possibility of baptism. They wanted baptism for their child, they wanted the Church, they wanted something which was difficult to articulate, as if language could not fully communicate the desire. Yet this presented a huge challenge: how can this initiation rite, this sacrament of the Church be presented in a coherent manner? The catechetical process has changed somewhat from the one described in the early Church. How might we, however, on behalf of infants and young children, understand the full magisterium of the Church, the power of God's grace through the Trinitarian marking of Father, Son and Holy Spirit upon their heads?

To a large extent, these questions have to be left for further reflection. I was concerned, however, that the family of the baptized – the parents, godparents and friends – were to respond to the promises, the affirmation of faith and the commissioning with conviction. The liturgy of baptism, its signs and symbols of oil, water and light, help explain something of the wonder of the event. The key element in my explanation centred upon people – those who offer a welcome and those who were being welcomed – for baptism expresses this pattern of inclusion at its heart. On a 'baptism Sunday' when we welcomed families to our Eucharist and the baptism within it, the church was alive with energy (and not a little noise). These occasions, highlights of any ministry, nonetheless raised certain questions. Was the meaning of baptism conveyed well enough to these newcomers and enquirers? Had I been true to the mission of the Church?

Mother Church

The vocational calling of baptism, be it infant or adult baptism, is a sign of membership into the sacred community called the Church, not only of the church today, but the cloud of witnesses that have gone before us, those who have given us this holy inheritance. The word Church comes from the Greek, εκκλεσια. Two words combine to create the meaning. εκ means 'out of', 'from' or 'away from' and the verb καλεω means 'to call', so Church is 'to be called out' of an assembly, congregation or gathering. To be a member of the Church, to be baptized, we are called not to stay still, but to move, to journey outwards wherever the calling is taking us, presumably into the place where God needs us to be, to the people that we need to be with, to the place where one's 'deep gladness and the world's deep hunger meet' (Buechner, 1973, p. 119). The mission to God's children is, I believe, the context of our 'gladness' and the world's 'hunger'. In baptism the child is called out of death and darkness across the borderland of faith into a new life in Christ. For the child, the

Church plays an important role here as parent: 'Mother Church', listening, holding, discerning, correcting, guiding. Mother Church holds the gift of faith in her hands. It is through the love, integrity and skill of the parent that this gift might be offered as a vocation.

To accept the baptism of a child who is unable to make a decision of faith, one understands that the child receives the mark of baptism with and through the community of faith. This is not an individual decision but a faith event which has been long in its gestation through the prayers of generations past. Just as John is fulfilling his vocational role according to Isaiah, so the newly baptized is performing his own vocational role according to their faith community, Mother Church, past and present. Our Christian identity cannot be bound up by a single event in time:

> Baptism is a reality whose meaning has to be discovered at each stage of a person's life, whether it is a young person appropriating the implication of his or her baptism in infancy, an adult making their baptism their own in all the complex developments of a human life, or a mother or father discovering Christ anew in the responsibilities of parenthood.[13]

Baptism requires us to discover its nature, purpose and significance throughout our Christian journey. We need to draw upon our pilgrim's manual to recontextualize the enormity of this calling, a calling which is founded upon trust. The child emerges from the baptismal waters as the embodiment of divine life. In this rite, the pilgrimage has been sacramentally marked. The adult–child relationship between the co-workers of Christ is established by trust – trust in one another but ultimately trust in God. Crossing the borderlands of childhood means enabling the child to discover and rediscover their baptism afresh and anew. Crossing the borderlands in the context of baptism also gives opportunity for the Church to be the guardian of discovery, of the exploration of faith. Mother Church is situated, like John the Baptizer, in the borderlands of faith, upon the frontier where the grace of God is called upon. John was the forerunner of the one to come, Jesus. John was a man of sacrifice and it is this example of sacrificial love that is axiomatic in building the Church of today. We, the adults, the ones that go before our children, must take full ownership and responsibility for the faith which we inherit and ultimately pass on. It is a gift to be received, opened and shared.

Chapter 4

Infancy and Early Childhood

It was Christmas morning. Exhausted and light-headed, unable to move from the shock of my ordeal, I looked up. Wide-eyed and alert, our new baby, just minutes old, gazed around the room, his breath audible and expectant. Still dark outside, he seemed captivated by the great shaft of light that beamed from the hospital lamp. In the minutes that followed, he would constantly return to it, his silence palpable, clothing us all in the miracle of his new arrival.

This new infant had made a pilgrimage indeed. Crossing the boundaries of birth into life, of darkness into light, in those defining moments that shape us all, I felt I was given a brief glimpse into another world: an understanding of the place that we have come from; of what it is to 'celebrate God's creation' and 'journey homewards to God' (Paynter, 2002).[1]

There is nothing easy or sentimental in this homecoming. If we view the journey sentimentally, then we are likely to slip up, and we will not be open to the possibility of discovering new terrains, new parts of ourselves. The extraordinary pain of child-birth – the belief in those final moments that the agony is almost too much to bear – is something I shall never forget. Bound by the present moment, it was as though the fragile thread that binds my own identity was pulled into a new existence. Like it or not, be any good at it or not, I would never be able to think of just myself again.

Identity in relationship

Childbirth is a baptismal experience. Literally born from the mother's waters, the infant's entry into life is a life–death encounter, one which embodies the extremities of both pain and joy. This is a borderland experience: through this experience both mother and child are called into a living relationship. Its primeval beginning marks out the unseen pilgrimage of the mother–child dyad in which all emotions, all depths of being have the potential to be revealed and transformed. And yet, both research and instinct tell us that this relationship does not begin with birth but with conception itself as, for the duration of pregnancy, the mother's mood, feelings, diet and lifestyle, her whole system in fact, exist in a symbiotic and dependent relationship with the unborn child (Gerhardt, 2004, p. 67).

From a faith perspective, this relationship is not two-way but three-way: the child is born into relationship with God. This is formalized in the rite of baptism where God identifies the child within the Body of his Son. Just as God as Trinity (Father, Son and Holy Spirit) shares life in mutual relationship, so too the child is called into mutual relationship with the community of believers called the Church. In this chapter, I shall consider how the developmental landscape of infancy and early childhood is enriched by an under-standing of baptism. Drawing on various psychological models, I shall argue that, when we bring together theological and psycho-logical thinking about childhood, this is not some dry, academic exercise, but one which provides us with the tools to a radical rethink of nurturing and protecting a child's identity itself.

*　　*　　*

Until recent decades, the infant's unborn identity was shrouded in mystery: gender, details of size, the potential for disability, all these and much more were utterly unknown. Now, in an age when consumerists' needs top the agenda and our culture is ingrained with a disposable mindset, our attitude to the sacredness of life is constantly being compromised, and this attitude is so endemic that we have to fight to contradict it. When I was pregnant with my first child and attended my initial maternity appointment at a large

London hospital, I categorically stated that I would not be taking up the option of certain tests, for example to find out the likelihood of having a baby with Down's Syndrome. Despite this, however, before I could intervene, the midwife had glanced at her chart and, regardless of my wishes, read to me, deadpan, the statistic for women my age likely to have a baby with Down's Syndrome. It was my first personal experience of how we judge and categorize one another, not least our children. The spirit of competitiveness and success – that is, a fear of fragility and 'failure' – is paramount from the moment a child is conceived. Twenty-first-century Britain has its own agenda about what a child's identity should be.

The many potential complications involved with pregnancy illustrate the long journey a mother and unborn child have to make before safe entry into the world is possible. Furthermore, complications do not of course necessarily stop at birth, but can be manifest in neonatal difficulties, a child's disability or chronic illness, either immediately or subsequently apparent. Where all has gone well, however, the rapid development of an infant during the first weeks and months of life is testimony to the discoveries and frustrations that are essential for an infant to move forward and build relationships with the outside world. With each new development – first smile, first sounds, meaningful eye contact, grasping a toy, sitting up unsupported, pointing, crawling, standing, walking, talking and so on – a new aspect of an infant's identity is revealed; revealed, that is, in his increased ability to respond to, explore and relate to the world.

These developments or 'milestones' each mark a frontier of their own: some are crossed almost without anyone noticing; others are heralded with enthusiasm and expectation like the dawn of a new era. As a clinical psychologist who has worked both in child and adolescent mental health and with children with special needs, I have never taken these frontiers of childhood for granted. Each new stage, each new pilgrimage, brings with it its own wonders, concerns, expectations and dilemmas. Each new stage contributes, therefore, not only to an infant's identity but also to an infant's relationship with others: 'Individuals are not self-generated or self-maintained. Born with a unique genetic endowment, their individuality is shaped and maintained through their relationship with others' (Ryle and Kerr, 2002, p. 40).

In infancy and early childhood, a child is dependent on his carers for everything. Not only must an infant's physical needs be met; the quality of the emotional relationship between the primary carer(s) and infant is paramount. It is through these core relationships that the infant will establish whether or not the world is a safe and satisfying place, and whether people can be trusted or not (Herbert, 1989). This is, according to Erikson, a key task of infancy: the development of 'basic trust' in others.[2] An infant's sense that people can be trusted is essential to his development and well-being.

It is a deeply uncomfortable truth that these early relationships are likely to have lasting effect.[3] The way in which infants learn to relate to their primary caregivers will go on to inform the way in which they relate to themselves, others and the outside world in later life:

> In early life this potential self is a bit like a seed planted into the garden of the family. Using this image it's easy to see that its growth and development is bound up with the nature of the soil and its environment … Inevitably some seeds will be planted in an acid soil when their growth is much more suited to alkaline; others may be pruned too early as their shoots are only just beginning to grow; some will land on stony ground. Some seeds, which perhaps have the potential to develop into peaches or pears, experience alienation when those caring for them are trying to raise oranges or apples and their own pear or peach nature goes unrecognised and unfulfilled.
>
> (Wilde McCormick, 2008, p. 7)

An infant's future identity is therefore, to some extent at least, shaped by the identities of those that care for him. It is during these early months and years that the parent can feel tugged and pulled in all directions, between desires of the 'self' and desires of 'other' as a new sense of identity emerges. In this way, the balance of the self–other relationship between parent and child is constantly being questioned and put to the test. From a faith perspective, this is the core test of our baptism: are we, as parents, godparents, as a community of faith, ready to respond to and foster the baptized? Are we ready to turn to Christ, to submit to Christ, to come to

Christ? (CW).[4] When we say 'yes' to these vows, do we actually mean it? Do we really know what we are letting ourselves in for?

A shared pilgrimage

Nothing in the world prepares you for parenthood: for its sheer intensity of highs and lows; for its non-stop, round-the-clock incessant demands; for its relentless routines and utter unpredictability; for the cruel, very real possibility of weeks, months, years even, of tortuous, child-inflicted lack of sleep! For my part, I embarked on it with unerring naivety, falling flat on my face as soon as I heard my baby cry. 'Why's he crying? What do I do now?' I would ask during the course of those first months, words that toppled my pre-maternal fantasies of myself as mother, creating in me a sense of ambivalence about my own status: an untold love and joy, on the one hand, combined with a sense of inadequacy, on the other. My own identity had, it seemed, been swapped overnight for another. This feeling was not unique to me but is, in different ways, shared by countless mothers, fathers, parents or carers of all descriptions. We cannot know it – we cannot begin to know it – but, when we cross that frontier of parenthood, we are entering a new landscape altogether, one in which we will, if we are prepared to look closely, discover our own strengths and weaknesses and find out new thresholds, utterly unimaginable until then, of joy and pain.

From a baptismal perspective, the question presents itself: how might we enter that landscape and 'walk with [our children] in the way of Christ? (CW).[5] As modern adults in a modern world, is this language just too obtuse, too 'holy' and difficult to grasp? Or might it have modern meaning after all? It seems to me that, if we are prepared to stop and explore the rite of baptism, infant baptism has the potential of 'being a map', not only theologically but psychologically also. That is, just as in baptism it is the role of parents, godparents and the whole community of faith to prepare the way for a child's spirituality to develop and emerge with God's grace, so too from a psychological perspective, a parent's role is critical in helping determine a child's future self. The Church has, therefore, at least in theory, a deeply systemic view of the child, one which understands the child's place in a broad picture of relationships and meaning. Theology and psychology come together as each places value on the system of relationships that the child inhabits.

'Sacred trust'

In our concern to care for children, we are not asked to be perfect,[6] but we do need to be adults that can be depended on, that can be trusted. This notion of trust is central to the Good Childhood Inquiry, which invites all adults to think of children as their 'sacred trust' (Layard and Dunn, 2009, p. x). The word 'sacred' is critical here. It demands of us to hold in mind not only a child's emotional needs but, integral to those needs, their spiritual core: that is, the sacredness of their life's journey; their unique identity that is of God.

This sacredness does not come with trumpets or banners but exists in the everyday of parenting, teaching, living, working or simply being with children. When an infant reaches approximately eight months of age, he generally goes through a period of 'separation anxiety'. This anxiety can coincide with a child's increased mobility – typically, his ability to crawl. As he discovers the ability to move away from his parent, he can start to sense the fear attached to this distance, and will want to return to his parent's side. A variety of attachment styles have been hypothesized and explored, including avoidant, ambivalent, disorganized and secure attachment.[7] Where the attachment between child and parent is secure, the parent represents a 'secure base' (Bowlby, 1969) and the infant, understanding that his parent is 'emotionally available' (Gerhardt, 2004, p. 24), will feel free to wander off and explore once more.

Central to a child's development of trust is the emotional learning experience that, although a parent figure might absent themselves, sooner or later they will return and respond to their child's call. 'Here I am,' 'Here I am,' I find myself repeating when I've risked disappearing out of view just that little bit too long. The phrase, repeated from parent to child, has of course strong biblical echoes, and recalls those Testament figures, new and old, ranging from Adam and Jonah through to Mary, who tussled with this phrase (*Hineni* in

Hebrew) before responding 'yes' to God (see Radcliffe, 2008, p. 33). For those figures that do respond 'yes' to God, the words articulate an absolute trust in God the father, a faith based on a relationship in which God's sacred trust in humanity is repeated back to him and given voice. One can assume that the words 'Here I am' would not be uttered if the speaker in question did not have a strong sense of whom they were addressing; that their audience (God) was in fact a 'secure base'; unconditional and constant and yet, always listening, always responsive, always active.

In a very different way, when a mother speaks the same words to her infant, she is hopefully instilling in her child that same sense of constancy and unconditional love, however flawed, however human, steeped nonetheless in divine potential because we all are created in the image of God and, through the course of our life's pilgrimage, seek to journey back there. While, therefore, the words 'Here I am', spoken from mother to child, are apparently commonplace, their consequences are anything but: when repeated and acted on, they represent the continued affirmation of the relationship between parent and child; the essential knowledge that, even when the parent is apparently out of reach, they are in fact available all along. It is through these early experiences of separation and reunion, however brief, that a child's trust in others is tested and, where a secure base is offered, realized. From this base, a child's identity is fostered and strengthened, enabling them, one hopes, to provide that same voice – that same 'Here I am' – to future generations.

'Rupture and repair'

In order to provide our children with a secure base, as modern-day parents we would no doubt find the task of parenthood easier if we were somehow able to draw on a more ancient understanding of identity: namely, where identity is defined in relationship to others and not to oneself.[8] To do this, we need to be sensitive readers of our children, empathic but not intrusive responders to their needs and desires. We need, in other words, to respond to an infant's desire for interaction when called for, and pull back when not called for, thus allowing the infant to experience what is known in the developmental literature as 'rupture and repair'.[9] This is in direct contrast with its counterpart, 'chase and dodge', in which the mother fails to read the infant's signals that he is ready to withdraw and instead becomes overly engaged in the interaction. These cycles of interaction, which last no more than 30 seconds, are thought to underpin an infant's early experience either of 'something getting better' or, alternatively, of something in which the infant experiences unresolved discomfort and which is ultimately disruptive to his emotional development (Douglas, 2007).[10]

In essence, these seemingly innocuous cycles of interaction help prepare the infant for the dilemmas and challenges of later life. As adults concerned to facilitate children's spiritual development without imposing it, we would do well to consider these different patterns of responding evident in interactions between mother and infant. The overwhelming message is clear: you can't start soon enough recognizing and respecting a child's identity, and this recognition is evident in the quality of communication and reciprocal interaction between parent and child.

The developmental notion of reciprocity has implications for a child's spiritual as well as emotional journey. A sensitive parent or church is one which will allow its children to explore their faith through a model of 'rupture and repair' and not by 'chase and dodge'. In other words, doctrine and beliefs should not be imposed on our children's identity, causing them perhaps to avoid the very thing we wish to endorse. The journey of faith is not a plateau but is full of peaks and troughs. By fostering our children's innate desire for reciprocity, we set them up for a mature understanding of faith, one in which they might discover their own relationship with God, their own highs and lows, expectations and disappointments. In a church, therefore, where reciprocity underpins people's relationships, space is created not for a holy few but for a community of pilgrims who, coming together either regularly or irregularly, will search out that sacred place to which we and our children are travelling. The start of this journey is formalized by the rite of baptism, a rite which celebrates a child's relationship to others and ultimately to God.

Cloister children

The rite of baptism has no real meaning for our lives, and certainly no meaning for our children, if it starts and ends as a symbolic act. The challenge, not only for parents and godparents but for the whole community of faith, is to remain alive to one's baptismal vows; to enable those vows to be extended throughout a child's infancy and early childhood right through to adulthood; to recognize that an infant, born in the image of God, has the potential to grow ever more into God's likeness, to journey home. The promises we make together at an infant baptism can, however, come under serious threat when either our own or other people's children leave infancy behind and the next developmental period, known as early childhood, comes into view.

The early childhood years (approximately eighteen months to four years) are frequently characterized by melt-downs and temper tantrums; by wanting more independence but not always being able to achieve it; by frustration and by other people's reactions. As a child's sense of self and identity emerges, so too does his behaviour. This behaviour is often put to particularly good effect in church as a flurry of letters and articles in recent years in *The Church Times* will testify.[11] 'Are we going to the dark church or the light church?' my sometime four-year-old once asked when I announced one Mothering Sunday that we would be going to church. I groaned inwardly. These words were a clear forewarning that the hour or so that lay in store was not to be easy. While I do not remember my exact response, I do remember that the question sat uncomfortably with me. This was not the kind of spiritual wonder I had once anticipated fostering in my children: a deep dislike of church, backed up, it seemed, with experience.

This type of experience reached a particularly low point one Sunday when, on holiday, we decided to visit the local cathedral. On arriving with all three children and immediately identified as tourists, it was politely explained to us that a service was about to take place. We responded that we had in fact come to attend the service. We were shown to our seats by one of the sidesmen who, friendly enough, suggested I could always take the children for a walk around the cloisters during the service. I really did not know whether to laugh or cry. Not two feet into the building, the children and I were already being reminded of a child's place in this centre of worship – on the edge somewhere, away from the action: 'cloister children' I shall call them. It did not take long for our fifteen-month-old to discover the echo, for our three-year-old to follow suit and for our five-year-old to lapse into a disappointed sulk. With literally not one other child in sight, we realized we had been over-optimistic to say the least and, after my best powers of persuasion, I left Gavin in the cathedral child-free. At one point he left to look for us but to no avail. When he returned, the sermon had already begun: its theme for that Sunday, 'Why are there no children in our churches?' At about this time I for one could have been found with my children in the cathedral coffee shop, sipping orange juice and eating flapjack. With three thoroughly contented children, all was well again. My three-year-old suddenly looked up and commented that he did not like 'that church', there were dinosaurs in it. His older brother quickly put him in his place: there were no dinosaurs in church, but there were churches for children and churches not for children – this was simply a *no children church*.

A child's notion of a 'no children church' is not easily reconciled with a more inclusive ethos of discipleship, and certainly not with our baptismal calling. But 'no children churches' have undoubtedly grown up because of a very real difficulty of managing children's behaviour in church, of understanding how best to include them, and therefore failing to include them in any real sense at all. In this context, a child's difficult behaviour becomes a dilemma, to say the least. And yet, with my psychologist's hat on, I cannot resist turning the spy glass on children's behaviour in church more closely and asking the question not so much *how* should children behave in church but rather *what* is their behaviour communicating? In other words, from a behavioural perspective, what triggers the behaviour in the first place and what factors can be seen to be maintaining or reinforcing it?

I shall call the child in my scenario 'Ned'. Ned is two and a half years old, it is Sunday, and his mother has decided to take him to church. At first, all goes well. Ned occupies himself in the 'children's corner' with some drawing and his mother relaxes. After a while, Ned grows restless. The first hymn has been sung, everyone has sat down, nothing much seems to be happening. He approaches his mother with his drawing and says something just that little bit too loudly. Ned's mother responds as positively as she can and Ned returns to his drawing. After another few minutes, however, art and Ned have really had their day. One packet of raisins later, he starts to knock his chair against the table. People turn round to see where the noise is coming from. Not all looks are disapproving but they are looks all the same. That's better, thinks Ned, at last, some attention. Buoyed up by the success of his intervention, he knocks the chair again, louder this time. More attention. The behaviour, tried and tested in a whole range of scenarios, is taking its full effect. Ned's mother approaches him and rebukes him further. This is perfect. Just when Ned was feeling ignored, utterly excluded from everything around him, an opportunity for conversation arises – the subject (his behaviour) might be negative, but it's better than no attention at all. He is told to keep his voice down or he will be taken out altogether. The long-awaited reward is in sight. Ned lets out a penetrating scream and his mother, fully demoralized at last, removes both herself and her child from the service. The liturgy can finish in peace.

From a behavioural perspective, the pattern of Ned's behaviour is easily identified. This pattern is best summarized as what is known as the 'ABC' of behaviour.[12] First, the A (or Antecedent), in other words, the trigger: Ned feels bored and excluded. Second, the B (or Behaviour): Ned is disruptive, makes a noise and so on. Third, the C (or Consequence): Ned's behaviour is reinforced by the responses of those around him; initially he receives some much-desired attention from neighbouring members of the congregation and latterly he is removed from church altogether, the greatest prize of all. In fact, next time, Ned is very likely to skip the preamble altogether and cut straight to the chase. Why hang around making a slight noise which only a few people notice when the full-blown melt-down has the greatest and most immediate effect?

The pattern is all too familiar and clearly many factors are at play. While I am not suggesting that parents do not take responsibility for their children's behaviour in church as they would hopefully expect to do in any other environment, parental discipline is not what interests me here. Too often it seems, children's behaviour in church masks a much more perennial issue: our desire somehow to silence or exclude children so we can get on with the business of being 'spiritual' ourselves. If children are not invited to belong to church, to feel included in the community of faith of which they are an essential part, then how can we expect to foster their sense of identity within the corporate body of Christ? Without that sense of identity, of actual belonging, why should children behave in church? Or, to reframe the question more positively, perhaps if a child identifies with church, finds a place in which he belongs, then hopefully his behaviour will communicate a different message, one in which he feels both heard and held? These questions guide us towards a model of Church in which behaviour is not managed but contained, in which the quality of the relationship between Church and child is everything.

Church as container

It was Easter Sunday. Sitting in an enclosed pew in a packed church in the Lake District with my children, I listened with both awe and wonder as children were actively invited to make as much noise as they liked during the service, and wander freely. Parents were not to worry. This was Easter. We were here to celebrate the risen Lord.

Surprised but delighted, I turned to my two older boys who, to my amazement, seemed actively engaged in what the vicar had to say. The service ensued. Shortly after the confession, children were able to attend the crèche or Children's Church, according to age or inclination. Some did, others didn't. My youngest, just walking, was content to wander: round and round we went, exploring the side chapels as we did so. Those children that had left the service rejoined us for Communion. As the final hymn struck up, I looked down it: all three, in their own way, were singing. They were not alone. This was the mystery of Easter. Despite the huge number of children in church that morning, their noise or wandering had not intruded at all. In fact, I had found that I had been able to focus better on the worship and the liturgy than I had in a long time. It seemed that the vicar had, consciously or otherwise, performed what they would call in strategic family therapy 'a paradoxical intervention'.[13] In other words, somewhere in the process of the children being invited to make as much noise as they liked, to wander freely and to feel included, it seemed that both parental anxiety and children's behaviour had been contained, fostering space for a more positive pattern of relationships between parent and child, Church and child, and parent and Church.

I am not, sadly, suggesting that all a worship leader need do is stand at the front of the church each Sunday and, by inviting his younger members to make as much noise as they like, reasonably hope for the opposite, not least because the church we attended also had several other structures in place to include and welcome the children. But, that aside, there is a profound message here, one which speaks above all about the relationship between the 'container' and the 'contained'.

I would now like to consider how an understanding of containment, first devised by Bion (1962), might better inform our ideas about the role of the Church in its fostering of Christian identity in childhood. The concept originated with the relationship between mother and infant:

> When all goes well, containment is a fundamental of what goes on between a mother and baby ... Babies with mothers who can take the panic out of their anxieties, eventually take into themselves some version of a mother who can manage – who can get hold of something emotionally without being knocked off balance by it. Eventually the baby takes into itself ... the mother's capacity to tolerate and manage anxiety – her own and her baby's.
> (Garland, 1998, pp. 109–110)

In other words, for a mother to be able to contain her baby's feelings, she has to be able to manage her own. In doing so, she will hopefully pass onto her child a huge gift: the gift of understanding, implicitly at least, that difficult feelings can be tolerated and that disaster will not win the day. In my experience, the process does not happen overnight but occurs through a gradual awakening of one's new self, one which reconciles the disturbance to one's former identity with a sense of calling to the new; which understands relationship to be everything, a far cry from what the Good Childhood Inquiry termed 'excessive individualism'.

Through the process of containment, the infant is understood to internalize his mother's capacity to think and reflect: 'Internalising the mother's capacity to think about something creates the internal space, or internal container, in which things can be thought about' (Douglas, 2007, p. 38). This process of internalization has implications also for the relationship between Church and child. If children feel listened to in church, that is understood, appreciated and included, in time they are more likely to internalize this 'capacity to think'; that is, they too will start to think, to reflect and to wonder as they grow and develop. If church can, therefore, be an environment in which children's feelings are contained and their ability to think is restored, this will lead to more settled and contained behaviour; the seeds will potentially be sown for a strong and lasting Christian identity. The church and its community of faith – where Church is the container and the child is the contained – will become 'a good enough mother' indeed.

A church built in water

When a church fails to understand what is meant by containment, it is in danger of failing to understand the identity of a child in a community of faith at all, of neglecting its baptismal vows altogether. The child becomes an object which can at best be manipulated in an effort to keep quiet, but any thought of their own internal world, one which provides a powerful expression of their core spirituality and which is frequently manifest in their play (Nye, 2006), is cast aside completely. It is all too easy to underestimate a child's innate sense of faith and wonder. As Rebecca Nye has observed, 'children's spirituality is erratic: one moment profound, the next almost forgotten'.[14] As adults who cannot help, it seems, focusing on children's *behaviour,* we tend often to notice only the 'forgotten' parts and fail to notice those moments of utter profundity, carried out with an unconscious ease known only to children; those moments, in other words, when a child's innate relationship to and sense of God is manifest.

I was given a chance insight into one of these unseen moments in my children's lives one bath time. They all three had taken their places in the bath and were busy with a whole series of bottles and various toys. They were particularly industrious that night – in fact, they had been for several nights now – but I had not given it much thought. On announcing it was time to get out, the sense of injustice was immediate. They were building a church, I was told, and had not finished yet; it had to be finished that night. I looked at them, all three. Even the youngest, who had been equally industrious, apparently inspired by a shared sense of purpose, looked perplexed. I relented. Pleasure all round. This time I listened in. Somewhere, with half an ear, I had been listening for several days, but I had not taken it in until now. The eldest was the architect of course, the other two mere labourers in the overall design.

They were mixing concrete, I learned, lots of it. The task needed to be finished that night. It was Sunday tomorrow. The words took me almost by surprise. Yes, I thought, it was Sunday tomorrow. Gavin would be taking school chapel but, as a family, we would not be going to church. I could not face it, especially not on my own with the children. I looked down at the bath and its muddy water; tirelessly scooped and poured with all the imagination of childhood, this was faith in action. As I pulled out the plug and watched the water drain away, I told myself that I would try to remember this moment; that, when Sundays came and went and the children moaned about church, or perhaps we just avoided it altogether, that they had in fact built a church of their own, not one visible to the adult eye, but real enough to them, and one which flowed unfailingly from the waters of that first baptism.

A church built on wonder

An imaginary church built in water speaks powerfully of a child's unique expression of faith, of an innate spiritual identity, all too easily overlooked. Even as adults who actively want to foster children's faith, this oversight can happen simply through misconception or our own lack of imagination, hence the *Church Times'* leading caption on the front page one week during 'The Year of the Child' – 'Please, God, no more colouring'.[15]

I received a timely reminder of what it is to underestimate a child's innate sense of God when Gavin and I began life at our previous church where Gavin was parish priest. Wanting to move Children's Church forward in some way, but unsure really how to do so, we called in the Diocesan Children's Advisor to help us with thinking about building on the already existing 'Sunday Club'. She helped us focus on a real fundamental of children's ministry: namely, that when children leave for Children's Church, they are not being dismissed 'to get on with their own thing' but rather are being invited to continue with the liturgy themselves in a different but connected place. Following this initial discussion we acted on the advice, and from thereon the children were asked up to the altar after the Confession and each was given something to hold (a candle, a bible a small holding cross) with which they would then process out.

The church hall was integral to the church itself, meaning that, as we all left the main body of the church behind us and entered the hall, the small altar we had set up (a children's table with a green cloth[16] on it and the 'storytelling rug' in front) was immediately visible. As we processed out for the first time, I remember feeling concerned that I had not explained what the children would need 'to do'. But before I had time to explain anything, the children, all aged between three and ten, had instinctively moved in silence towards the makeshift altar and placed their objects before it, kneeling down on the 'story-telling rug' we had laid out. It was a true 'Godly Play'[17] moment, one which gave me a lasting insight into children's inbuilt sense of awe and inherent spirituality, their reverence for what is sacred, their innate understanding of God.

Perhaps this is why I feel so desolate sometimes when I pull one of my own children, kicking and screaming, away from church, and take solace in the silence outdoors. When Gavin and I left parish ministry in London, we did so with just our first child in tow; he was not yet two years of age, and we had scarcely experienced firsthand the trials and tribulations of taking a child to church. And yet, there is another way, as Jerome Berryman's inspirational work on 'Godly Play' testifies – a way in which children's voices are listened to and nurtured, in which their feelings are contained and responded to, and their first attempts at initiation, their pleading for reciprocity, is not left unnoticed. As I write from a borderland place – still searching for home – a psychological reflection on the sacrament of baptism seems to offer one way of re-entering and reconceiving the place of infancy and early childhood; of reminding ourselves not only of our children but of those promises we once made on behalf of our children, to bring them up in the practice of faith, to welcome them into the place that will, we hope, bring both us and our children closer to God.

Integrating Mind and Spirit (Part 2)

Identity

The emergence of an infant's identity depends upon their relationship to significant others. In both theological and psychological terms, the adult is required to hold the child in mind, to see outside themselves, to place the needs of others before their own. In baptism it is the role of parents, godparents and the whole community of faith to prepare the way for a child's spirituality to develop and emerge. This resonates with a developmental understanding of infancy and early childhood in which significant adult-child relationships pave the way for a child's future sense of self and identity. Just as parents and godparents need the support and encouragement of the Church to bring up their child in the practice of faith, so too parents and carers require the support of a wider community – family, friends, professionals and other bodies – to respond to and nurture their children's physical and emotional needs.

In essence, baptism offers a model of good practice in which adult–child relationships are fostered and allowed to flourish because an adult's sense of identity is not bound up in a self-centred perception of 'I' but includes also an other-oriented sense of self, in which identity is shaped by relationship to others and ultimately by relationship to God. If the Church is to fulfil its baptismal promises and adult–child relationships are to be truly reciprocal, the child's identity, presence and belonging must be valued as integral, not limited to sections of church life or, worse still, shut out and put on hold until the child better conforms to an adult's perspective of church-appropriate behaviour. In baptism, the child is invited to deepen the Church's knowledge of God's image. Only if this invitation is genuine can the Church offer a living and authentic model to contemporary adults about how we might relate to and respond to the children of today.

Called to respond

When we hear the words of the Commission at a child's baptism, we hear the calling of the Church. We are reminded of the baptismal promises made on our behalf by others. We are also instructed to go out into the world and put the promises we make today on behalf of children into practice. In reflecting upon the following passage, how might you respond personally or corporately (for example, as a family, school or church) to its calling?

The Commission within the Rite of Baptism (CW)

We have brought *these children* to baptism knowing that Jesus died and rose again for *them* and trusting in the promise that God hears and answers prayer. We have prayed that in Jesus Christ *they* will know the forgiveness of *their* sins and the new life of the Spirit.

As *they* grow up, *they* will need the help and encouragement of the Christian community, so that *they* may learn to know God in public worship and private prayer, follow Jesus Christ in the life of faith, serve *their* neighbour after the example of Christ, and in due course come to confirmation.

As part of the Church of Christ, we all have a duty to support *them* by prayer, example and teaching. As *their* parents and godparents, you have the prime responsibility for guiding and helping *them* in *their* early years. This is a demanding task for which you will need the help and grace of God. Therefore let us now pray for grace in guiding *these children* in the way of faith.

Part 3

Formation

The Borderland Children

We are the borderland children
Bearing our sticks and staffs for the journey,
Hidden from eyes glazed in slow furnaces,
Catching the sky in our hands whilst
We roam. Kingdoms of clouds slip
Through our fingers, manna immerses our
Minds as we run hurling hope like spears
To enter the palaces, riding wings of the wind
And heat of the sun.

We are the borderland children
Tramping our march over crossings,
Seas parting, pausing to peer in dark
Caves fissured by tides,
Dabbling our sticks in sand puddles
And climbing the crests side by side.

We are the borderland children
Called by creation, outpacing fear to the
Hinterland. Do not search for our seats
In the temple, don't garrison heartlands,
We are breaking boundaries of long
Grasses, shadowed woods, stepping through
Streams to wash our tired faces, approaching
A place deep in the criss-cross of frontiers,
Locked in a landscape of longing
And God.

Dallin Vines

Chapter 5

Confirmation

A slap in the face

Confirmation might well be viewed as 'a rite looking for a theology'.[1] Unlike the sacrament of baptism, confirmation cannot claim direct biblical precedence, but has developed as a sacramental rite to validate the baptized in their continuing faith journey. In simple terms, confirmation can be seen to be the point at which the person of faith reaches a decision to 'take on' the vows made on his behalf at baptism. The promises which were made through the parents and godparents are now taken as a personal commitment of a maturing faith. The godparents are released from their duty of care, at least in an ecclesial sense. However, with the various Christian denominations adopting different theological positions and pastoral practices, the rite of confirmation is something of an ecclesiastical minefield. While it is not the purpose of this chapter to study these theological practices in detail, an initial brief overview will highlight something of the complexities at play.

Within the Roman Catholic Church, children are generally confirmed during adolescence, following a period of instruction, but are permitted to receive communion prior to this (i.e. in the pre-pubertal years). The Anglican theological position, by contrast, is very much 'work in progress'. While some dioceses are promoting something akin to Roman Catholic practice, thus enabling baptized children (or adults) to receive the Eucharist before confirmation, more typically individuals within the Anglican Church do not receive communion until they have been confirmed.[2] The Orthodox position varies once more, whereby the confirmation (or chrismation) is administered directly after the rite of baptism in accordance with apostolic practice witnessed in Acts 19:1–7 and 1 John 2:20. At the risk of being overly simplistic, it would seem that the Church has created this sacrament, but does not quite know what it is for. Is it a rite of entrance to the Eucharist? Is it a rite signifying physical and emotional maturity? Or is it a rite centring on spiritual formation, signifying an individual's readiness to reconfirm their baptismal vows and become a fully commissioned disciple of Christ?

From the perspective of a father, a priest and a teacher, this theological perplexity might actually help those involved with the task of the formation of young minds and spirits. Although it would misappropriate the rite of confirmation to label it simply as a rite of passage for children or adolescents, there is something about this rite which speaks of transition, of borderland territory, of social, physical, emotional and spiritual awareness. This is a messy business, one which requires patience, time and enormous reserves of energy, for this is the path of initiation, the formation towards Christian maturity. The rite of confirmation may well prove to be ambiguous but the goal remains the same: to present to our young people the Gospel and the Christian faith, and to invite them to share fully in its life, as disciples of Christ.

Each year at school, after collecting the names of the children who have asked to be confirmed, I wonder whether this forthcoming passage of time and learning will provide them with a deepened identity of their sacred selves. When my confirmands stand before the bishop at their confirmation many weeks later, they wait with eagerness and trepidation. They understand that the bishop will lay his hands upon their heads and convey the Holy Spirit upon them. They have been instructed that he will anoint them with a perfumed oil named Chrism, a sign of the kingdom, to strengthen the disciples of Christ in their formation. They anxiously anticipate a 'slap' across the face, or perhaps, in truth, a tap.[3] This 'slap' has legendary roots. Many suggestions have been formulated regarding its original purpose. The first is that it represents a type of exorcism, another that it replaces the kiss of peace with a prophetic warning that much will have to be endured in the struggle for Christ's kingdom. Still another legend has it that, in previous centuries, the diocesan bishops (who were and still are the 'ordinary' ministers of the sacrament of confirmation) were largely absent from their pastoral duties. London was their locus, for these Lords of the Church were required to attend proceedings in Parliament. When they returned to their dioceses on horseback, they confirmed people 'on the move' as they returned home. The laying on of hands was replaced by a less than holy slap in the face!

This, then, is the story of confirmation, a rite that has changed and developed through many of the Christian centuries. Through the lens of this particular sacrament we might be able to discern something of the spiritual integrity that is inherent in the lives of our children, an integrity that leads to maturity of mind and spirit.

Seven Up!

'Give me the child until he is seven, and I will show you the man.' This well-used aphorism, purportedly coined by St Francis Xavier of the Jesuit order, is the raison-d'être of the social documentary, 'Seven Up!' In 1964, the film-maker Michael Apted chose a number of seven-year-old children from a variety of social, economic and ethnic backgrounds as the focus of an ongoing social and political enquiry. The programme attempts to test the hypothesis whether the child of seven might in fact demonstrate significant traits, perceptions and behaviours which antecede its adult path. The nature–nurture dichotomy is explored at seven-year intervals through the unfolding observations of Tony, Suzy, Simon, Bruce, Lynn, Nick, Sue, Paul, Andrew, Jackie and Neil. The next series, due to be shown in 2012, will be entitled '56 Up!' The simple, storytelling structure of the series is both intriguing and insightful, fast-forwarding and rewinding through significant passages and events as each individual plays, builds, deconstructs and builds again philosophies, world-views, beliefs and relationships. This whole complex of human experience develops upon the screen from childhood through adolescence into early adulthood and beyond. The profound message of 'Seven Up!' reflects the fragile nature of each life's journey and the resilience of these people.

Sitting one early spring afternoon in the grounds of Ty Mawr convent, situated in the border country just outside Monmouth, I observed my own 'Seven Up!' documentary. I had organized a pre-confirmation retreat to this place of quiet solitude and rare beauty which involved a nature walk, a Godly Play story about the days of creation, an attempt at *lectio divina*[4] (from the Gospel used in the confirmation service) and the composition of prayers (used as inter-cessions for the service). The boys had been joined by their female peers from the girls' school, and were being instructed about their first task of the retreat – a nature walk, a sensuous lesson in looking, listening, touching, smelling and tasting. The confirmation classes had come to an end and we were all preparing, as best we could, for the rite of confirmation and for the invitation to the eucharistic feast. That evening, these boys and girls would be confirmed by the bishop through God's heavenly grace, anointed by the Holy Spirit, empowered for God's service. Sitting and observing, I could not help but wonder where these young people had come from and where they might they be going. If I were able to fast forward this documentary to the next seven years, who might they become? What of another seven-year step in time, what might have become of them then?

These children, tasting and testing the grounds of God's world, were entering a life-time's calling: 'God has called you by name and made you his own' (CW).[5] Where might this calling take these children? Perhaps away from this border place, this springtime, alive with the sights and sounds of new possibilities. Certainly their formation would be tested, possibly at school the next day, should they be asked about the retreat or the confirmation itself. How might they describe these experiences to their peers? Might the unfolding of each individual's particular story also demonstrate something of fragility and resilience?

The calling of any individual to make a life's response to God and his Church is a calling that requires nurture and encouragement. For confirmation is a corporate responsibility for all the covenant makers involved in bringing these young people to this particular stage in life. Some will struggle to stay in the fold of the Church; some will feel they have failed; others will return and make it their home. Throughout all of these stages of life, these servants of God require time, grace and prayer. For these are the building blocks of emerging discipleship and the essence of the Christian documentary marked by the Spirit.

Where is home?

I remember very little about my own confirmation, although some details do remain. I can still recollect the sense of ceremony, of anticipating the bishop's arrival, of being made to feel special, wanted, even belonging. My preparation was given by my parish priest on a one-to-one basis. He visited my parents' house for one particular session of instruction. I remember seeing him arrive in his car from the lounge window and, knowing that my parents were out, I decided to hide from him, wanting to escape this school-after-school which involved such dry subjects. My older brother answered the door. It took me some time to build up the courage to reappear and attend the class. The fact was that the idea of confirmation confused me; I didn't know where I fitted in or indeed what the Church was in which I was to confirm my faith.

As one who now prepares others for confirmation, these memories do evoke a sense of realism in my current objectives when recruiting a new group of confirmands. I do remember what it feels like to be lost among the strange creeds and doctrines, of wondering how to relate to the world of covenants and commandments. To my surprise, my spiritual quest, rather than being thwarted by such an arid grounding was, in fact, enabled. It was in the midst of the struggle to reconcile my boyhood sense of self with the institution of the Church that I encountered a question which has been the basis of my vocation: 'Where is home?' The question may provide a signpost for others as they cross the borderlands of childhood. Certainly it has implications for the confirmation candidates when asked, 'Are you ready with your own mouth and from your own heart to affirm your faith in Jesus Christ?' (CW). Through the course of their preparation, the confirmands have at some conscious level to grapple with their identity. In other words, where might they situate themselves in relation to the Church? Is it a place of homecoming or might it be too close to the edge of their known landscape?

The experience of living close to border territory where danger and distrust exist is not only a challenge for contemporary childhood. The prophet Jeremiah's formation became manifest at a time when identification with his mother religion was in constant flux. His fellow religionists had been exiled from the centre of their faith, the

Jerusalem Temple, and been banished to a foreign land. Jeremiah's calling from the womb was one of many in the prophetic tradition of the Old Testament. It seems that this divine calling knew no bounds or limits. Just as Jeremiah was called *in utero*, so also was the prophet Isaiah: 'The Lord called me before I was born, while I was in my mother's womb he named me' (Isaiah 49:1b). Here we have a purposeful and involved creator who is calling and commissioning his creation to carry out his work. This is a God who crosses the borderlands of childhood, who seeks out his image in others. Jeremiah was 'only a boy', which surprisingly did not disqualify him from the task set by God, but was the basis of his commissioning:

> Now the word of the Lord came to me saying,
> 'Before I formed you in the womb I knew you,
> and before you were born I consecrated you;
> I appointed you a prophet to the nations.'
> Then I said, 'Ah, Lord God! Truly I do not know how to speak,
> for I am only a boy.' But the Lord said to me,
> 'Do not say, 'I am only a boy';
> for you shall go to all to whom I send you,
> and you shall speak whatever I command you.
> Do not be afraid of them,
> for I am with you to deliver you, says the Lord.'
>
> (Jeremiah 1:4–8)

God uses Jeremiah, the son of the priest from the priestly tribe of Levi, living in the suburbs of Jerusalem, to speak on behalf of him. Jeremiah cared little for the overt workings of religiosity. His prophecies centre upon the work of the heart. Here was a true borderman. As he grew, he recognized that the place of his origin, Judah, was a frontier territory, that Jerusalem was a marked city but, most importantly, a sacred place. Squeezed between the might of Egypt and Babylon, God's land of promise was to be invaded and desecrated. Yet Jeremiah was able with a child-like simplicity to issue a corrective for his people. He implored his nation to realize both the opportunity and threat which the frontier represented. Not only was Jerusalem in danger because of its geography, but also because it had forgotten its true nature, its real identity, its vocation to and for God's children. Jeremiah had been called by God to pose the sacred questions, 'Who are you?' and 'Where is home?'

Living on the border

The chapel in the life of a school has a paradoxical function. Situated at the centre of the school day, it nonetheless remains on the edge of activity. Like many aspects of the school, the chapel and the chaplaincy are compromised, even squeezed, in order to accommodate the complexities of timetabling and extra-curricular pursuits. All the same, the chapel, at least at Monmouth School, remains an integral feature. Much effort and prayer have been invested in order to offer this sacred space as a core resource in the formation of mind and spirit. The chapel has been reordered and furnished with brave art by devoted benefactors. For many former students who revisit the school, the chapel is the first port of call. They recollect that, despite their disillusion or even boredom with the place during their school years, they remember their time at Monmouth in the first instance of walking through the chapel doors. The chapel remains the constant in school life where much around it changes from one period to the next as one term rolls into another. The challenge of chaplaincy is to present the Gospel in a way that is at once relevant, coherent and ripe with integrity. This is the spiritual challenge – living on the border – overseeing different outlooks and behaviours, receiving scepticism and enquiry, providing time and space in the noise and bustle of an institution of learning.

Each year, at the end of the Michaelmas term, I seek to recruit boys who are interested in being confirmed. The annual project starts with a publicity campaign explaining what confirmation means. I write a pastoral letter to parents in Advent, explaining all that has happened in the chaplaincy over the past year and what we hope to achieve in the New Year. Confirmation preparation is integral to the year's activity. By the beginning of the Lent term, we are ready to start a twelve-week course leading to the confirmation service shortly before we break for Easter.

The boys who respond to the recruitment process tend to offer a very wide spectrum of faith, knowledge and experience. Some will not have been baptized. Many will not be familiar with the significance of the Church's liturgical times and seasons. The twelve sessions, or confirmation classes, have been fought for against a range of competing lunchtime forces, including sport and music. Each 30-minute session is valued time, sandwiched between lessons, lunch and extra-curricular pursuits. In practice, this time is even more reduced as the boys arrive late and others leave early for other 'protected' activities. The boys' attitude when we meet for the first time is one of ambivalence. In past years, I have experienced a lack of motivation or interest and a resistance to adapt to a different way of learning. Initially alarmed by these typical reactions, I attempted to experiment with the content and structure of the confirmation course. Having started with a traditional and rather formulaic offering of doctrine, dogma and belief, in time new incarnations appeared in an effort to achieve the right balance, to initiate thought and provoke enquiry. I wrote an article for the School Chaplains' Conference entitled 'The All-Knowing, The All-Singing, All-Dancing, All-Encompassing Confirmation course'[6] which denounced my previous attempts of trying to do too much: 'My greatest concern is that we place an intellectual impediment in the way of our young people knowing God with their hearts. The pedagogic relationship of student and teacher needs to be re-framed somehow.' I was starting to understand that, by turning the child–adult relationship on its head, by allowing God's grace and not simply human intervention, to do its work, we are better equipped to understand not only a child's spiritual formation but also our own.

Teaching the teachers

My article not only portrayed the complexities of living on the border for both student and teacher, but also the child's innate ability to respond to God's call. This ability directly links to the story of Jesus as a young boy, probably of the same age as many of these confirmands. Jesus, most particularly in Matthew's account, was located in his Jewish and kingly heritage. The child Jesus was alive to all that had gone before him. He was receptive to the stories of past generations, the landscape of memories,[7] but he was also aware of the gift of faith that he valued so highly. The vocation of Jesus and all those who had contributed to the story of faith had been imbibed in wisdom. Wisdom is invisible yet proven throughout the course of human history. It is made tangible through the lives of God's chosen people and Jesus is the paradigm, the exemplar of wisdom, fully integrated in mind and spirit, even as a child:

> Now every year his parents went to Jerusalem for the festival of the Passover. And when he was twelve years old, they went up as usual for the festival. When the festival was ended and they started to return, the boy Jesus stayed behind in Jerusalem, but his parents did not know it. After three days they found him in the temple, sitting among the teachers, listening to them and asking them questions. And all who heard him were amazed at his understanding and his answers.
>
> (Luke 2:41–43, 46–47)

Jesus, the child, was marked. The festivities had ended, the sacrifice had been made, religion had done its work, the families returned from their pilgrimage. Yet the child was called to continue the festival, the 'festival without end'.[8] Jesus, the child, was marked, the Holy Spirit was upon him, his Father's voice calling, gently leading him to his vocation's task, crossing the borderlands and entering the places of power. And so he found himself in the Temple, the frontier place between earth and heaven, teaching the teachers. Through the mist of burning incense, Jesus revealed something of God's desire for humanity, a desire that seeks a response – to travel across borders and boundaries and discover the precious gift of holiness present in all of God's children.

This early Temple incident (not unlike Jesus' final visitation as an adult) led to anxious questioning. Jesus provokes a response in the heart of his hearers. The response is not often comfortable, but nor is the sacred place to which we are asked to return. Jesus asks, 'Why were you searching for me?' For this child had marched a path to holiness, to a place that he calls home. Jesus' kith and kin were literally searching for God, not that they fully understood the subject or nature of their search. The irony of the question 'Why were you searching for me?' should not be lost. It is clear in any vocational quest that we constantly lose sight of that for which we are searching. In terms of parenting, teaching, nurturing or caring for children today, our search is equally confusing. Anxious questioning becomes a necessary precursor to understanding. In my task as a father, a priest and a teacher, I am intrigued by the formation of the boy Jesus, especially by the marks of his divinity. Following in his footsteps the borderlands also provide the marks and signs of vocation abundant in the lives of the heroes of our faith.

Browsers versus explorers

Jesus was a natural explorer not only of his known world but also of mystery and the invisible realm of existence. Not only did Jesus have a sense of otherness, of spiritual encounter, but he also had a real sense of home and homecoming. The parable of the prodigal son comes to mind here. Jesus was prepared to go to the very edge of his received religion, Judaism, and at times venture beyond its borders and thresholds. Like many explorers, Jesus risked his life in his search. Yet this was not an exercise about pitching resilience against survival. Jesus' example was to demonstrate the nature of spiritual formation, to explore life at all levels from different perspectives, in other words, to live life in all of its fullness.

One of Britain's greatest explorers, Sir Ranulph Fiennes, the first man to visit both the North and South Poles, recently publicized a website 'Freeze Frame', dedicated to the history of exploration.[9] 'Freeze Frame' exhibits an incredible array of photographic images documenting the extraordinary exploits of the polar explorers. Fiennes observes that the website allows browsers to become explorers. Reflecting upon this observation, I wondered whether it might be possible to categorize the current generation of young people into those who are prone to browsing and those who are more naturally inclined to explore. The inference is made in the context of the age, a time in which the internet has affected 'the way that we do things', especially in commerce and industry, in family life, and in education and training.

As a teacher of children from ages eight to eighteen, I experience the profound effect that the internet has on children's learning. It is very difficult to focus students' research on books. Information has never been more easily accessible. While this is a great gift, the information often leads to saturation as the mind is flooded by distractive and sometimes destructive paths of enquiry. Although the internet, if used in the right way, is a wonderful educative resource, it can also be a divisive tool, one which blunts an exploratory approach to a given subject. Many students regard cutting and pasting from a website as a legitimate response to a question set for homework. Fiennes might categorize this type of behaviour as belonging to the category of the browsers, those who are happy to have a simulated experience rather than an actual experience of life. The way that we are prepared to experience the world and all that it offers is, like many other commodities today, given over to choice. The cut-and-paste generation, those who choose not to immerse themselves in an integrated search of mind and spirit, are further enticed into a virtual world through video games and internet sites. This virtual world is one that has been created and is maintained by adults. A significant challenge for today's adults is therefore to encourage a spirit of exploration and independence in childhood. It seems that there exists a resistance in contemporary society to going to the primary source, to travelling to the place of initiation of thoughts and beliefs. The temptation to live this cut-and-paste experience is increasing. The danger is that the real learning, which comes from physical, intellectual and spiritual exploration, is being subsumed under a culture of superficiality. Many fight shy of crossing the borderlands:

> We live in an increasingly risk averse culture where we are limiting our children's out of home experiences because of fear of harm. However, risk taking is a developmental imperative of childhood – young people and children will always want to explore boundaries by taking risks, and they will sometimes play this out, at home, in the digital world with many parents unaware of this. In the same way that we teach our children how to manage 'real world' risks, for example crossing roads, in stages and with rules, supervision and monitoring that changes as they learn and develop their independence, we need to engage with children as they develop and explore their online and gaming worlds.[10]

When confirming the young, it is inevitable that both browsers and explorers will be recruited, and this is the challenge of the sacrament, to transform the browser into an explorer and to ask the explorer to travel further in the quest of truth. What of the subjects of this year's confirmation? To what extent are they browsers or explorers? How might the rite of confirmation, the anointing with the oil of Chrism, the working of the Holy Spirit, transform and call them towards the borderlands of enquiry and beyond? For these are the questions which test spiritual formation and its component parts – wisdom, integrity and bravery. These marks of vocation are displayed throughout the Christian centuries in every land, demonstrating the universal character of discipleship. In this land of Wales, and more specifically the borders where I write today, a Celtic hero who lived 1,500 years ago continues to encourage others to explore the possibilities of living the Christ-life: his name, Dewi Sant.

Dewi Sant

Be joyful, and keep your faith and your creed. Do the little things that you have seen me do and heard about. I will walk the path that our fathers have trod before us.[11]

These are the words that St David purportedly preached during his last celebration of the Eucharist in 589. These words could have been written for a rite of confirmation for they sing of Christian virtue, of joy and obedience, of listening and searching. David's life was chronicled some 500 years after his death by a monk named Rhigyfarch. By delaying committing his life's work to paper, much of David's biographical detail could legitimately be described as legendary. Nonetheless, here we have a sixth-century monk, abbot, bishop, archbishop and teacher of the faith who was a missionary to many pagan people and places. David established twelve monasteries and countless churches, and renewed monastic life to boot. His own monks in the principal monastery near Menevia, today known as St David's Cathedral, were schooled in David's dedication to work and pray:

By his rule he obliged all his monks to assiduous manual labour in the spirit of penance; he allowed them the use of no cattle to ease them at their work in tilling the ground. They were never suffered to speak but on occasion of absolute necessity, and they never ceased to pray, at least mentally, during their labour.

(Butler, 1936)

Legend goes further, describing David as 'aquaticus' or the water drinker, demonstrating how discipline and a rule of life served as being the foundations of his vocation.

The Chapel at Monmouth School recently commissioned a mosaic triptych of Dewi Sant. Designed by a local ceramicist, Dee Hardwicke, the mosaic beautified the redundant space of a blocked-in window. The mosaic serves as a life-size reflection upon this patron of Wales. David is seen blessing those who sit before him in the chapel pews. He is situated among the local hills, the Sugar Loaf and the Skirrid (the Holy Mountain), which locate David in this border landscape of the Black Mountains. A river runs through the scene emphasizing the importance of water, explicitly baptism, in his and the Judaeo-Christian story. Twelve fish are running upstream towards the altar at the east end of the chapel. Finally, a beautiful white and gold inlaid dove hovers over the scene as the Holy Spirit oversees the work of David, but also the work of David's brothers and sisters of faith today. At the dedication of the mosaic, Archbishop Rowan Williams meditated upon David's life with some members of the school's community:

I'm sorry to have to tell you this, but in the long run, the person God wants us to be is a saint, he wants each one of us to be holy in our own way. Holy, not in the sense of three foot off the ground and no use to anybody, but holy in the sense of honest, faithful and visionary. A person who makes things happen around them: good things, Godly things. Holy in the sense of being faithful to Jesus Christ and all that he lived and died for. That's all God wants of us.[12]

David's life was one given up to being a follower, not of any whim or fashion, but of a wisdom which was not of this world but of God's. We hear something of this wisdom in the Old Testament:

> Whoever holds to the law will obtain wisdom. She will come to meet him like a mother, and like a young bride she will welcome him. She will feed him with the bread of learning, and give him the water of wisdom to drink. He will find gladness and a crown of rejoicing, and will inherit an everlasting name.
>
> (Ecclesiasticus 15:1–6)

There is a flavour of permanence here, that wisdom, the cultivation of truth and understanding marks the world in which we live, marking it for the good. Perhaps this is a clue to St David's continuing appeal that, despite massive advances in science and technology, despite the huge changes to our patterns of living at school, at work, at leisure, we remember an ancient, impoverished, yet wise monk who saw the work of the Spirit from his position of ordinariness. So this is the life story of an explorer who illustrates knowledge through wisdom and bravery within the disciplined context of monastic life. Such a life resonates through time and space to the borderlands of childhood where we are reminded of God's permanence and our transience. Perhaps Dewi Sant's story and the stories of countless other saints might offer assurance to those being confirmed in the faith. The Christian faith comes from a common inheritance lived by 'honest, faithful and visionary' people.

The Sacrament of Invitation

Let us return to our 'Seven Up!' documentary. The final activity of the confirmation retreat focused upon writing prayers that could be used for intercessions in the confirmation service that night. The children read out their prayers in the chapel of the convent. They were startlingly direct and honest. It was decided what prayers would be used; these were transcribed and taken away. The remaining prayers were left at the altar as an offering to the community at Ty Mawr for their hospitality but also an offering to

God. I returned to Ty Mawr a month later to celebrate the Eucharist. The sisters had collated the prayers and compiled them into a little book. I was told that each day one of the children was being prayed for by the community. They felt that this was an important exercise, to keep that particular group of young people connected in some way with the community and, through the community, into the heart of God. This of course is the essence of monastic life, to bring the world to the attention of God. The sisters of Ty Mawr were also carrying out a role which is crucial, especially among the young; that of welcoming. Children need to be welcomed into the faith, not patronized. They need to feel that they are deserving of their place at the table. With a quiet, prayerful method, the sisters are doing just that, providing a space for the confirmands to fill in their own characterful, creative way. At such times, in the context of the calling of young people, the established community, parents, sponsors, priests and elders, have a duty of care to welcome all-comers into the Christian life. Confirmation is integral to the whole community of God. The sacrament of invitation, the giving and receiving of faith, is a testimony to the care that exists in the Christian family.

Confirmation may be 'a rite looking for a theology' but it is also a rite that needs to be recognized and celebrated. The sisters of Ty Mawr, situated in that border place, accompany the young and walk with them in the best way they know how – through prayer. Each year the children reflect upon the confirmation experience and each year they name the retreat and the convent as being the highlight. This, then, would be the concluding scene from my own 'Seven Up!' documentary: the children laying down their prayers in the convent chapel and in so doing expressing their very own personhood, offering their faith, hope and love. The words of the bishop ring out in anticipation of the confirmation service that evening: 'God has called you by name and made you his own. Confirm, O Lord, your servant with your Holy Spirit' (CW). Despite placing the confirmation service annually in the Season of Lent, it seems that Easter arrives early with the candlelit procession of young people at the end of the service receiving the congregation's applause. These individuals have been prepared in the Lenten desert, the place of austerity and silence. Perhaps this is a good grounding for them, that they understand something of the nature of border territory: it

94 *Called by Mind and Spirit*

is not safe, comfortable or permanent. This hard environment of learning may inculcate a sense of desert wisdom in which they are better able to discern the nature of their calling. Ultimately it is God's Spirit that excites the confirmands. It is God's Spirit that encourages them to leave the Lenten desert to fulfil their own public ministry. Despite my own misgivings and doubts, the Holy Spirit was able to shape and form these borderlanders, and invite them homewards.

Chapter 6

Middle Childhood

The young tree

The playground in which I find myself each day offers a panoramic sweep of middle childhood. The playground belongs to the infant section of our local primary school and is connected by a simple path to its junior counterpart. Built by the council nearly a decade ago when the schools were first amalgamated, the path acts as a concrete link between what once represented two distinct worlds. In their reception year, the children, aged somewhere between four and five, make their entrance into this new world via one door. Seven years later, as their primary school years come to a close, they leave it by another. Middle childhood is, it would seem, characterized by its very own 'Seven Up!' experience.

Given that middle childhood (approximately four to eleven years)[1] covers such a huge expanse, the term itself seems somewhat overinclusive. As a developmental stage, it is relatively neglected by the psychological literature. As adults, however, we neglect this stage at our children's peril. For these years are nothing if not critical, marking as they do a whole host of changes, physical, cognitive, emotional and social. During this period, a child's thinking about themselves, about others and about the world around them becomes more sophisticated, and this in turn affects their social skills. Peer relations become increasingly intense, often surviving ruptures on a daily basis; and the number of adults in a child's world also grows, thus expanding the range of influences on their development.[2] Given all of this, it is scarcely surprising that research over several decades has found that a child's abilities and experience during the middle childhood years will significantly contribute to their formation in adolescence and adulthood (Huston and Ripke, 2006).

The finding highlights the significant responsibility of adults entrusted to nurturing today's children. The experiences and environments with which we provide them – combined with our ability to step outside our own needs and consider theirs – are essential to their long-term growth:

> Just as the growth of a young tree is permanently modified by pruning or grafting, the growth of a child depends in part on the directions that the family, school, peer group, and other environments encourage or discourage from [in the middle childhood period].[3]
>
> (Huston and Ripke, 2006, p. 433)

The message is clear: these years are critical to a child's formation and have the potential to help or hinder development. For some, middle childhood is a stable time, building on the blocks already in place, offering new challenges in a consistent and safe environment. For others, however, these years are marked by instability: a change in school perhaps or home, a breakdown in the parental relationship, a bereavement of another kind, the possible reconstitution of one's family – factors which are not of course confined to any one stage of childhood but which are no less significant here.

Regardless of whether this period is primarily a positive or negative one, the expectations placed on the child – to read, to write, to form friendships and conform to social rules – are high, sometimes with little room for compromise. Within this context of expectation, it is all too easy to forget children's spiritual formation, to hold in mind that, irrespective of their literacy or social skills, the individual pattern of their formation is unique. In this chapter, I shall consider how the rite of confirmation might help us reflect on what it means to journey through middle childhood. In doing so, I am aware of an obvious tension between the age range of middle childhood and the more typical, higher age range of Anglican confirmands. As already stated, however, the purpose of the comparison is not to draw a literal connection between a sacramental rite and a developmental stage, but rather to consider how the formation of mind and spirit, expressed by the rite of confirmation, might help us reflect on ways of nurturing faith in middle childhood. I shall begin, therefore, by looking at one key aspect of preparing for this rite, as already discussed in the previous chapter: exploration and discovery.

The loss of Mighty Mac

Becoming human is just one crisis after another, as we break through into an ever deeper intimacy with God and each other.
(Radcliffe, 2008, p. 107)

It was the end of a particularly long day. I stood, shivering in the playground, counting the seconds until the door would open and the children, one by one, would tumble out like dominoes. It would be typical, I thought, that, when all I could think about was getting the children home, my child would be last in the cloakroom somewhere, still looking for his bag and coat. But no, I was in luck, there he was, practically right at the front. I could tell from his posture immediately that all was not well. When his turn in the line came around, he pointed towards me with an air of tragedy and started his descent down the path to where I was standing. The matter was soon made plain to me. He had lost his train, 'Mighty Mac', not any old train but his most favourite train of all. I sighed. This was not the smooth transition to the car I had been hoping for.

The scene was interrupted by a gaggle of boys, also from the reception class. Sam, always chief spokesman for the group, took charge. Having briefly summarized the situation, without so much as a by your leave he organized his cohort into some kind of a search party. This child, not yet five years of age, was apparently capable of turning a crisis of insurmountable proportion into an outing. The identity of the group was present for all to see. Peer pressure at its best was in full swing.

Very quickly, the boys were several feet ahead. The other parents and I did our best to hold them back, but in vain. Browsing was not on the agenda. Exploration of the most urgent kind clearly was. Off we went – pushchairs, siblings and all. We staggered down steps and made our way to the other side of the building. Here the playground stretched out onto a field – muddy and waterlogged, it seemed a far cry from the fenced garden which joined the reception classroom itself. None of us, it seemed, on leaving our children each morning, had realized the extent of their parameters. Willingly or unwillingly, we had dismissed them into a landscape wider than the one we had envisaged: one whose physical terrain would be explored and unearthed in ways known only to childhood, and whose challenges would change on an almost daily basis. Well, Mighty Mac was not found on that particular occasion but his disappearance was a lesson to us all: the importance of allowing our children to cross the borderlands; to learn to recognize, like Jeremiah before them, the opportunities and threats presented by borderland territory. Only by making the crossing for themselves will they come to understand the paradoxical states of crisis and recovery; of what it is 'to become human' and find out 'intimacy with God and each other' (Radcliffe, 2008).

Physical and spiritual exploration

Sam's initiative took both him and his peers, not to mention a small number of parents, to exploring a range of places, both new and unfamiliar. In the fifteen minutes or so that ensued, we watched our boys as they set about their exploration with renewed energy and purpose. Earth was dug, an old boat was inspected, even water weeds were given a cursory glance. In this way I stood idly by and observed how, in exploring their physical environment, these boys were engaging with so much more than a bit of mud and water. They had set themselves a task and, though the task had no satisfactory ending, the exploration and outcome was all their own. Had they been thwarted in this task, in one sense, so be it. But children must be given the opportunity to explore their environment in a way that intrigues and challenges them. Exploration is, very simply, a touchstone of middle childhood. If we hinder our children's desire to explore, we risk impeding their development at all levels. This is because the 'main psychosocial dilemma' of middle childhood is, according to Erikson (1959/1980), 'initiative versus guilt'. Carr gives an account of this dilemma as follows:

When children have developed a sense of autonomy in the pre-school years, they turn their attention outwards to the physical and social world and use their initiative to investigate and explore regularities with a view to establishing a cognitive map of it. The child finds out what is allowed and what is not allowed at home and at school ... Children who resolve the dilemma of initiative versus guilt act with a sense of proportion and vision as adults. Where parents have difficulty empathizing with the child's need for curiosity and curtail experimentation unduly, children may develop a reluctance to explore untried options as adults because such curiosity arouses a sense of guilt.

(Carr, 2006, pp. 29–30)

In other words, an adult's influence on a child's development during middle childhood is critical. It treads a fine line between supervising and attending to a child's world, on the one hand, and allowing the child to explore and find out for himself, on the other. As a child's ability to explore his world increases – physically, verbally and imaginatively – he becomes vulnerable to new discoveries, new fears and new crises. Erikson (1959/1980) argues that this expansion goes hand in hand with the child's increased moral awareness which, not yet fully formed, is susceptible to being both quickly forgotten and overly literal:

The child now feels not only ashamed when found out but also afraid of being found out. He now hears, as it were, God's voice without seeing God ... This is the cornerstone of morality in the individual sense. But from the point of view of mental health, we must point out that if this great achievement is overburdened by all too eager adults, it can be bad for the spirit and for morality itself.

(p. 84)

In brief, as adults we are required to foster a child's sense of right and wrong without imposing it; to allow him to recognize and amend his mistakes without 'overburdening' him with a sense of shame. What is more, while I understand Erikson's reference to God here to be at a symbolic level, I cannot help but be intrigued by his frame of reference. It would seem that a child's sense of God, be it implicit or explicit, is associated with his growing sense of moral awareness. The rite of confirmation, in particular preparation for that rite, seems to offer some insight here. In understanding confirmation, perhaps we can better understand what it means to foster a child's psychological awareness: 'The purpose of confirmation preparation is to ensure that those who are confirmed have a proper understanding of what it means to live as a disciple of Christ.'[4] The statement reveals that, when an individual is prepared for confirmation, in one sense he is presented with a clear set of parameters, handed down by the faith which he inherits. But within these parameters lie endless possibilities of mind and spirit, both visible and invisible to the casual eye. How that 'proper understanding' might be defined is clearly a limitless task; and yet the invitation to confirmands to explore and understand their faith for themselves is a helpful reminder of what it is to be a child progressing through middle childhood – ripe for discovery but in need of guidance also.

Just as preparing for confirmation is about fostering an individual's spiritual awareness, middle childhood is, as Erikson describes, a period in which the child develops an increased moral awareness of the world that he inhabits, the improved ability 'to investigate and explore regularities with a view to establishing a cognitive map of it' (Carr, 2006, p. 29). In a psychological sense, this exploration does not occur unless the parent, teacher or other significant adult provides the child with the space to explore and discover for himself – a space which takes risks but which knows its boundaries all the same, which continues to hold the child in mind while allowing the child to develop away from the adult figure, testing the world in which he lives and finding out what he can and cannot do.

This understanding of middle childhood has much to say in an age when we are concerned about achieving a helpful balance between protecting today's children on the one hand, and giving them the freedom to explore for themselves on the other. The task of achieving this balance cannot be underestimated. Nonetheless, the fact remains that, in order for a child to develop, his opportunity to explore the environment is essential. This appears to be happening less and less in modern Britain. In recent months, 'Natural England' has voiced its concern that children are no longer being given the freedom to explore the natural world as they once were, that instead we are bringing up a generation of 'cotton wool children'. Stephen Moss, speaking at the launch of the 'One Million Children Outdoors' programme at the Natural History Museum's wildlife garden, commented on the perils of disallowing our children the opportunity to explore: 'Concerns over child safety are understandable, but if children can't get out and explore the natural world, we run the risk of raising a generation of "cotton wool kids" whose experiences are defined by websites and computer games.'[5]

It is increasingly apparent, therefore, that many of our children are missing out on what it is to explore and discover the outdoors independently. In doing so, it is possible they are protected from certain difficulties, from mini crises of one sort or another. But these 'crises' are central to a child's formation, psychological and spiritual. We need to be mindful that, as adults responsible for children, we are not simply responsible for their physical and emotional well-being. Integral to this care is their spiritual development also: that is, just as children must be encouraged to explore their physical environment, so too is it essential that their thirst for spiritual exploration and discovery is fostered. David Hay expresses this concern vividly in the seminal text *The Spirit of the Child*:

> The adult world into which our children are inducted is more often than not destructive to their spirituality ... You will have seen it often enough. Children emerge from infancy with a simplicity that is richly open to experience, only to close off their awareness as they become street-wise. To be open is to be vulnerable. Its contrary is 'to know the score', to know how to look after yourself in a hostile environment.
>
> (Hay with Nye, 2006, p. 33)

As struggling disciples of Christ – broken and hostile on the one hand, willing and open on the other – we are called upon not to sit back in a spiritual slump, but rather to provide our children with a landscape of exploration and discovery. The terrain ahead is at times likely to be unpredictable. It will lead not only to our children's discoveries but also to our own; not only to a better understanding of those we are called to care for but also of ourselves.

Core beliefs

According to Erikson, in the final phase of middle childhood, the child is required to understand the importance of 'industry' or work: 'The child must forget past hopes and wishes, while his exuberant imagination is tamed and harnessed to the laws of impersonal things – even the three Rs' (Erikson, 1950/1995, p. 232). These words, written almost sixty years ago, do not make for easy reading and are as relevant now as they were then. A child's need to engage in work comes with a high cost attached, the potential for 'inadequacy and inferiority' (Erikson, 1950/1995). In brief, the child who struggles either socially, academically or in terms of sports (or all three) is liable to suffer from a sense of failure, low self-esteem and poor motivation to achieve, not just in childhood but in adulthood also (see Carr, 2006, p. 30). The connection here between an individual's experiences in middle childhood and his adult self is critical. As adults, we need to understand that our failure to nurture our children's self-esteem and sense of well-being is likely to have devastating consequences in the future, not only to the mind but to the spirit. We need therefore to establish regular opportunities for our children in which they feel a strong sense of their own worth.

Cognitive behaviour therapy (CBT) is one of several psychological models which understands the connection between the quality of a child's early experiences and their psychosocial functioning in later life. Simply put, the model is based on the assumption that how an individual thinks will affect how he feels and that this in turn will impact on how he behaves.[6] As adults, how we think and react to situations is in part determined by 'core beliefs' which we hold about ourselves (e.g. 'I am a good person'; 'I am worthless'). These core beliefs stem from early childhood experiences. We need to be mindful, therefore, of the experiences with which we provide our children as these will help determine the beliefs they hold about themselves, both now and in the future.

The concept of 'core beliefs' does not, however, only lend itself to a psychological way of thinking. A more radical perspective of the CBT model might incorporate our spiritual beliefs also. In other words, when we seek to provide a child with good early experiences, we must not separate mind from spirit and spirit from mind. We need instead to integrate a psychological understanding with a theological one. When we seek to foster a child's well-being, to help them reach their own potential, we place value on their unique pattern of strengths, gifts and vulnerabilities which, from a Christian perspective, are reflections of the divine nature.

It seems to me that today's children are at high risk of internalizing a very narrow set of core beliefs about themselves. This risk is underpinned by the pressures and 'obstacles' they face, and returns us to the conclusion of the Children's Society Report: 'Most of the obstacles children face today are linked to the belief among adults that the prime duty of the individual is to make the most of their own life, rather than contribute to the good of others' (Children's Society Report Summary).[7] What strikes me most about this conclusion is the emphasis it places on the consequences of adults' beliefs on children. When a child is brought up to place worth on a very limited band of values (defined, for example, as tangible success or achievement), they are in danger of losing sight of deeper values, and this impacts on their whole person, both mind and spirit. Erikson is more than aware of the far-reaching nature of this impact:

> But there is another, more fundamental danger, namely man's restriction of himself and constriction of his horizons to include not only his work to which, so the Book [Bible] says, he has been sentenced after his expulsion from Paradise. If he accepts work as his only obligation, and 'what works' as his only criterion of worthwhileness, he may become the conformist and thoughtless slave of his technology and of those who are in a position to exploit it.
>
> (1950/1995, p. 234)

Erikson's 'theology' seems to have crept in again, be this literal or symbolic. His warning acts as a dual reminder: in restricting a child's development, we do not only hinder their psychological well-being, we also fundamentally place an obstacle between them and their primary relationship with God. Erikson's use of the word 'exploit' is not one we can gloss over. Certain questions present themselves. As adults in positions of care and responsibility, are we nurturing our children's needs or are we in fact exploiting them? How might we helpfully foster our children's self-esteem in a climate which pays so much attention to 'aptitude' (as defined by a very narrow set of parameters), to material things, to a desire for instant gratification? How, in other words, might we better enable our children to be 'happy' in the full meaning of the word?

This last question is explored from the perspective of adulthood by Christopher Jamison in his book *Finding Happiness: Monastic Steps for a Fulfilling Life*. Here he sets out a thesis in which adults are looking for a 'fake' happiness (he compares it with 'a fool's gold') and fail to see a more lasting and real happiness, one which has its roots in our spiritual formation, which ultimately belongs to God. This happiness cannot be 'tamed' or 'harnessed' but is open to an upside-down perspective of being which defies 'selfish' living and instead turns the focus on relationship, on community and on belonging.

This upside down perspective, expressed throughout Jesus' teachings, was evident at the Special Olympics 2009. When a young boy with special needs fell down during his race and started crying, the other children in the race stopped, turned around and went back to help him up. One girl with Down's Syndrome gave him a kiss, saying, 'This will make you better.' Then all the children in the race linked arms and walked to the finishing line together.[8] The story provides a powerful witness to the poignancy and beauty of common kindness, of discipleship and fellowship, of God's own humanity. The instinct and values demonstrated by these children resonate strongly with the overriding argument of the Good Childhood Inquiry: that is, where the prime duty of the individual is to contribute to the good of others. The example is all the more noteworthy because the children's behaviour was not taught or adult-led, nor was it dependent on particular cognitive abilities or so-called 'typical development'. Rather the behaviour was free of expectation, utterly unselfconscious and rooted in values that can scarcely be articulated. This is what 'teaching the teachers' is all about.

When we seek, therefore, to go against the tide, to recognize and foster our children's core spiritual values, it would seem that there is another way. Core beliefs, which are hopefully the foundation of our Christian beliefs, point to the very opposite of low self-esteem and poor self-image. At their best, these beliefs aspire to those attributes evident in the lives of the saints such as Dewi Sant, attributes of wisdom, discipline and faithfulness. This is not of course to say that, by having a faith, one is exempt from vulnerability, far from it. But our underlying faith, sometimes utterly barren, sometimes burgeoning, does help highlight each person's potential in the eyes of God. What is more, by invoking in children a sense of awe and wonder, a curiosity to explore and discover, perhaps we can respond to the *acedia* of our times in a way that is at once realistic and radical. Bit by bit, we can start to build in our society a new set of core beliefs and assumptions, one which challenges ideas of self-promotion, consumerism and instability as the inevitable by-product of modern living. In doing so, we will enable our children to cross their own internal borderlands – social, emotional, cognitive and spiritual – and so discover a landscape unique to them.

The borderlands of confirmation

The possibility of this landscape brings us full circle to the rite of confirmation in childhood: the opportunity for a child to explore his faith for himself and, if he decides he wants to, to reaffirm those promises first made on his behalf at baptism.

Against my parents' better judgment, but not against their will, I was confirmed at the peak of my own middle childhood, at the age of eleven. In truth, the decision to be confirmed had not so much been mine as my 'best friend's'. While I was happy enough at the thought of confirmation, I attended classes not really because I wanted to but because I feared the possibility of social exclusion that not attending might bring. I was thoroughly unprepared, therefore, for one girl in our class who seemed to be there because she genuinely wanted to be. She was always on time for classes, always seemed attentive and, what was more, she had a way of saying things that got me thinking, of rousing me, if only for a moment, from the sleepy confines of my introspections.

It was something of a shock when, in our final class before confirmation, the priest told us that this particular girl would not be attending the class today. She had enjoyed the classes very much and learned a great deal from them but she had decided she was not ready to be confirmed after all. We were all invited to consider the question for ourselves. I said nothing. How would I know if I was ready, I thought? If I did not know, did that mean that I was not?

The rite of confirmation was for me a borderland place. While I have not forgotten the occasion on which I knelt at the altar rail and received my first communion, I do not remember, I cannot imagine what I was thinking, when the bishop asked, 'Are you ready with your own mouth and from your own heart to affirm your faith in Jesus Christ?' (CW). Neither ready nor unready, willing or unwilling, I crossed the frontier of confirmation with an uncertain step and, though I did not know it, a decision made with a child's whim would provide me with my first real experience of what it means to cross an unknown threshold, to search out a spiritual home.

Comic Relief

I am aware as I write that borderland imagery seems to pervade the book; we scarcely seem able to stay away from it. Perhaps that is not surprising: geographically, we are writing from a borderland place; spiritually, we feel very much on the edge, of a church life, of a prayer life, of a life in which we feel able to root and nurture our children's own spiritual formation. These borderland experiences, painful because they demand that we live with uncertainty, do nonetheless have a way of opening ourselves up to new experiences.

When I sat down to watch 'Comic Relief' 2009, I did so with not a little anticipation. With the combined prospect of a celebrity edition of 'The Apprentice' and yet more from 'Gavin and Stacey' in store, the line-up looked promising. However, despite a week's anticipation and fund-raising events of different kinds, I was, I confess, far from prepared for the purpose and impact of the evening's entertainment: the unavoidable reality of poverty, tragedy and associated grief of families and children in Africa, a reality which is present not only when as a nation we tune in once a year, but which continues throughout the year and will do so for years to come.

We each of us have different thresholds, emotional, spiritual and physical, and these thresholds vary according to our individual differences, our past experiences and where we are at in our lives.

When it comes to witnessing another's pain, we are not asked to raise that threshold but rather to respond to it, to understand that the impact of what we are seeing or experiencing is a call to our better part not just to be but to act. It can be all too easy to ignore that signal, but sometimes a window into another world can take us unawares and, far from providing just a snapshot, gone in 60 seconds, that snapshot becomes a lasting insight into a part of oneself scarcely visited.

'Comic Relief' is bursting with such potential, particularly in its stories and images relating to children, and yet it is all too easy to eradicate the realities of other people's lives from our minds and then sit back again. Strong emotions are liable to surface, emotions of distress, empathy, hopelessness. These feelings do not, however, only belong to countries beyond these borders. They belong also to the borders of our own lives, to the lives of those children we are committed to nurturing and understanding. What will we feel when we encounter today's children, our own and others? What will we think? And how in turn will we react? Will we shake our head, think 'not good enough' and walk away? Or will we stop, take stock and consider what might be done to improve the lives of others, to provide our 'borderland children' with a different landscape, one which is not simply carved out in consumerism and competitiveness, but which knows a landscape beyond, one that is of God and inherited by all?

'Comic Relief' insights, whether they belong to our own context or another's, are, by definition, painful. The predicament of contemporary childhood – of what it means for a child to flourish and grow in a society which too often aspires to 'a fool's gold', which potentially stifles exploration and discovery – is the breeding ground for many such insights. These insights, where they relate to a child's distress and brokenness, or perhaps to their emotional withdrawal, their apparently numbed senses, can be both disturbing and painful, and are likely to raise a whole host of thoughts in us. These thoughts have of course infinite possibility but might well sound something like this: 'I can't help; there's no point; it will make no difference anyhow.' These thoughts immediately evoke a whole range of feelings: of distress, of being overwhelmed, of the magnitude of it all. Given that how we think and feel is inextricably linked to how we behave, it is no wonder that such insights can bring out a conflict of behavioural responses in us: to act and do, on the one hand, to close off and run away, on the other.[9] To turn our behaviour around in a positive way, we need to identify and challenge the negative thoughts which underpin our actions.[10] When such thoughts are successfully challenged and transformed – when we seize the day and those thoughts are transformed not only by ourselves but by an openness to God's grace – only then can we shake off our spiritual sloth, find a way of responding to today's children as well as observing, a way of transforming as well as empathizing.

Middle childhood, frequently neglected by the psychological and developmental literature is, a bit like confirmation, lacking certain clarity. Just as confirmation might be viewed as 'a rite looking for a theology', the vast expanse of middle childhood might equally be viewed as 'a period looking for a psychology'. And yet, middle childhood, far from being some kind of no man's land, not quite one thing or another, is a critical place where foundations already laid can either be reinforced or reversed, depending on the quality of experience, environment and relationships that occur during this time. A child's strengths and vulnerabilities, visible now to the interested eye, have reached a critical point. These years are highly formative. As a child leaves them behind, he ideally starts to understand that the world's parameters contain much more than the here and now, that the possibility for relationship and discovery is inherently paradoxical, open and limitless on the one hand, necessarily boundaried and structured on the other. Similarly, when an individual prepares for confirmation, he is asked to think outside himself, to understand that he belongs to a bigger entity than just his ego. In one respect, the parameters of faith know no bounds; in another, they are bound by a rootedness in beliefs which, first made on a person's behalf at baptism, are renewed by the individual himself at the time of his confirmation.

The shared task of confirmation and middle childhood is, I suggest, the potential for the young person to exist and perceive outside themselves, to transcend those limits not previously known to them. This task, begun in middle childhood and formalized by the rite of confirmation, is one that we as adults are called to consider also. The 'slap in the face' traditionally administered during confirmation has its metaphorical place in everyday living: it is a slap that will hopefully cause us to rise us from our 'spiritual carelessness' and bring us to our senses. The touchstones of confirmation and middle childhood – exploration, discovery and learning – must not be forgotten in adulthood if adults are to help and not hinder a child's spiritual formation. Whether we are watching Comic Relief or going about our daily lives, we are all asked, not forcefully but forcibly, to internalize those external images, of crisis, of breakdown, of humanity itself, in an unseen and silent part of us. These images, which speak of prayer, demand that we 'shake off' our spiritual sloth, that we do not forget that all children are our 'sacred trust'; that we each of us have a responsibility to see beyond the borders of our daily lives, not in order to drive ourselves to distraction, but so as to remember the unique gift that is life and the unique relationship that is of God.

Integrating Mind and Spirit (Part 3)

Formation

A child's spiritual and emotional formation is rooted in their capacity to explore the world. From a theological perspective, the process is formalized in the rite of confirmation in which the candidate is asked, 'Are you ready with your own mouth and your own heart to affirm your faith in Jesus Christ?' From a developmental perspective, the process comes vividly into view at the start of middle childhood as the child becomes better equipped to initiate their own quests and ventures. In doing so, the child encounters both joy and pain, crisis and recovery. In this context, it is the adult's task to provide the child with a framework, a clear set of boundaries. Within that framework, however, the possibilities are endless, and the child must not be curtailed in their curiosity but rather be allowed to find out the questions and meaning for himself.

As a rite of initiation, confirmation stands on the edge of the Church. Its meaning, its theology is still being worked out. Its key themes of exploration and discovery convey, however, the struggle of developing discipleship. By actively encouraging the child to cross the borderlands, to ask questions which intrigue, challenge and confront them, the Church invites and welcomes the young in their search. When prepared to learn from its children, the Church transforms itself into a place of renewal and regeneration.

Called to respond

The rite of confirmation actively encourages and commissions young people to explore their known world and develop a sense of godly wisdom. At such times the Church offers a homecoming to the young disciples of Christ. When we hear the promises that these children make at their confirmation we are reminded of their commitment to God's calling. In reflecting upon the following passage, how might you respond personally or corporately (for example, as a family, school or church) to its calling?

The Commission within the Rite of Confirmation (CW)

Will you continue in the apostles' teaching and fellowship,'
in the breaking of bread, and in the prayers?
With the help of God, I will.

Will you persevere in resisting evil,
and, whenever you fall into sin, repent and return to the Lord?
With the help of God, I will.

Will you proclaim by word and example
the good news of God in Christ?
With the help of God, I will.

Will you seek and serve Christ in all people,
loving your neighbour as yourself?
With the help of God, I will.

Will you acknowledge Christ's authority over human society,
by prayer for the world and its leaders,
by defending the weak, and by seeking peace and justice?
With the help of God, I will.

May Christ dwell in your hearts through faith,
that you may be rooted and grounded in love
and bring forth the fruit of the Spirit. Amen.

Part 4

Vocation

The Forest

From afar the forest looked a fearful place,
Dense foliage netting sunshine, darkening
It to midnight. Yet we must leave fields,
Buttercupped and drifting with warm
Breezes, to turn our cooling gaze
On sterner sights.

The trees watched us. We were trying
To follow the map marked out long ago,
Travel its path through strange country.
Were those archers stirring the shade,
Arrows eyeing our journey? The tracks
Were muddied and marred, tendrils
Scourging our faces, but the call that
Carried us breathed of our way
Lifting our heads to guide us.

Branches moved mouthing commands
From hunched shadows: make haste, turn
Aside, slake your thirst, seize tomorrow.
Then hurry! cried some, where echoes
Swooped down, hurry on, hurry on, oh
Please stay we begged but they turned
And were gone, dropping their sticks and
Their staffs as they fled.

We waited. Minutes drifted to hours
Whilst we rested and days gathered time
To garland our brows. Silence wafted
The forest wiping our faces to scatter each
Tear as we lay on the ground. At last through
Wide trees we glimpsed sight of the kingdom and
Arms spread in welcome to beckon us home.

Dallin Vines

Chapter 7

Ordination

Called alongside

To be called by mind and spirit is a feature of God's intervention with his created order. Through the patriarchs, the prophets and the kings of the Hebrew Scripture, to the disciples and apostles of the New Covenant, God calls. In terms of kingdom building, the New Testament records a particular sense of calling made up from two Greek words, παρα (para) meaning 'beside' and καλεω (kaleo) being the verb 'to call'. Literally meaning 'to call alongside', παρακαλεω (parakaleo) can also be interpreted as cheering on, exciting and encouraging. Used mainly in St Paul's letters to the new communities of faith situated in and around the Gentile world of the Mediterranean basin, this particular form of encouragement is a mark of care and nurture for those of a fledgling faith in Jesus, the Christ, the Saviour. In Rome, Galatia, Corinth and Ephesus, young Christians were cheered on and excited by the apostle Paul. These formative years in the life of the Church depict what it means to get alongside one another.

The Church's ability to 'call alongside' young people, to engage with them and have empathy for their trials and predicaments, will help determine their potential to find out for themselves who they are, to perceive their vocation in the fullest sense. Vocation, like identity, is therefore about relationship and in childhood the burgeoning relationship to peers, to significant adults, to the Church and to the world. 'The vocation of the child is to grow and develop and become a mature adult,' writes Elmer John Thiessen (2008, p. 391). The statement, which places childhood on a continuum with adulthood, is a timely reminder to adults of their responsibility to foster today's young, to 'call alongside', understanding that today's children are tomorrow's adults.

Vocation, from the Latin *vocare*, meaning to call, is defined as a divine calling not only into the Christian ministry, but a calling into any facet of God's purpose such as work, marriage or parenthood. The American theologian, Frederick Buechner, expands on this definition, defining vocation as 'the place where your deep gladness meets the world's deep need' (1973, p. 119). The call to the specific vocation of ordination represents a disciplined commitment to serve the people of God alongside Christ. To be ordained, then, is to live according to God's holy law, to understand that the world in which we are situated is sacred, it is of God.

I understand my vocation to be a priest in the Church of God, but this is not to say that I don't have other vocations to fulfil. Vocation is used here in its widest, most generic sense, of finding a place of fulfilment and purpose. It includes not only an understanding of one's gifts and strengths, but of one's vulnerabilities and brokenness also. As someone recently reminded me, 'God doesn't call the equipped, but equips the called.' Being ordained into the 'professional' ministry of the Church is but one pathway to vocation. The rite of ordination offers us a sacramental understanding of the nature of calling, but it is certainly not a definitive model; not all vocations are a calling into the religious life or ministry. Nonetheless, the signs and marks of Holy Orders provide a distinct pattern through which we can interpret and discern other forms of vocation which are no less important. The rite of ordination, therefore, represents something about service and the needs and fulfilment of the Church and the world.[1]

The rite of ordination is applied to the borderlands of childhood and vocation not as a literal frame of reference but as a guide. Clearly children are not permitted to enter into Holy Orders. All the same, ordination into the three-fold ministry of the Church, of deacon, priest and bishop, can help demonstrate the nature of recognizing and responding to God's calling. The rite gives authority to look upon the world with a different, even divine, perspective; it is to see God and his creation holistically. In this chapter, I shall consider how a theological understanding of calling might relate to a contemporary look at childhood from two perspectives: the perspective of young people growing up, and the perspective of those adults whose task it is to foster and nurture the young.

A festival of youth

A sense of vocation is flavoured with a feeling of excitement, an excitement that perceives the Christian faith to be dynamic, freshly interpreted, and above all practical (in accordance with tradition) for each and every generation. This is the 'dynamic of the provisional' that Brother Roger sought for his community of Taizé. The story of this ecumenical brotherhood provides a source of encouragement for the Church today. It is, as Pope John XXIII described it, 'a little springtime' in which the community has been called alongside young people in their confusion and anxiety and given them direction and purpose:

> You want to follow Christ, and not look back: will you dare to put your trust in the Gospel time and time again? Will you keep setting off anew, drawn on by the One who walks quietly beside you, never imposing himself? The Risen Christ is present within you, and goes before you on the way.
> (Brother Roger of Taizé, 2000, p. 9)

This festival of youth encountered on a Burgundian hillside has been the source of countless vocations. In my own experience, it was on this hill that the mystery of the presence of Christ became tangible in the silence and activity of a religious community. Since the time that its founder, Roger Schutz, arrived by bicycle at a near-deserted village in south-east France called Taizé in 1940, the calling of God has echoed from this place. The calling flowed from Roger's generosity, of welcoming others into a shared life. Roger initially protected Jewish refugees from the scourge of the Gestapo, putting his own life at risk. His family had experienced, through several generations, how war and conflict could break the heart of the human family. From his Protestant roots in Switzerland, he prayed and laid the foundations for a community life that would embody the spirit of the beatitudes: joy, simplicity and mercy. The Taizé community would grow and be shaped through reconciling Christians one to another in a parable of communion where everything is shared. The welcome that was offered at its inception was developed to embrace young pilgrims who had started to arrive on the hill. Each year, more and more arrived, questioning, prompting, searching. As the community of brothers grew in size so too did the vocation of this ecumenical order. Young people from all over the world would come to this hillside in their thousands, wanting to seek answers to questions, to journey deeper, to experience something of this festival of youth.

Taizé is a model of community which transcends young people's negative experiences of religion and their sometimes 'punitive images of God' (Nye, 2001a, p. 98). In its invitation and welcome of young people the Church possesses a rare gift, a place where individuals can find a place of refuge. The young are accepted unconditionally for who they are and are actively encouraged to be themselves and not try to be someone else. During a short stay at Taizé, it is tangible to see in the lives of the young pilgrims a quiet confidence developing as discernment replaces judgement. Curiously, the young people respond well to the religious discipline of the daily rule of prayer, study and work. The distinctive form of prayer held three times a day offers a meditative setting alongside the repetitive chants and the silence of the worship. Study involves a led Bible study by one of the brothers of the community, and small groups reflecting on central themes. Everybody has work to do and through these common tasks many friendships are formed. By the end of a pilgrimage to Taizé in which Easter is celebrated every Sunday, vocation too is celebrated; it has become the common language of all the pilgrims, excited and encouraged by the presence of the Spirit of Christ.

God calls us into relationships, as a collective, as a people, as a Church. The young are called to receive the Spirit's guidance and power. The Spirit's blessing gives the children of faith armoury to sustain their vocation in an embattled world that can at times be hostile to faith. The Spirit is present at Taizé, guiding, consoling, helping and intercessing, allowing the young to become vulnerable, to take risks, and to grow. Brother Roger describes this same Spirit as 'the breath of Christ's loving'. God comes alongside his children as he calls, encourages and excites us on our journey through the borderlands, a journey whose destination is called kingdom. Through a child-like trust, the community of Taizé displays a hope, a springtime, for the Church today. When we take our children seriously, when we are transparent in our response to their needs, they will respond to God's Spirit. The Church of the Reconciliation upon the hill of Taizé sings out this truth. The prayer echoes across the landscape, catching the breath of the young: 'Lead my people,' calls the Christ, 'you are to be the shepherd to my people.'

The kingdom builders

'When were you called by God?' The question reverberated around the student body. We were ordinands, about twenty-five in this particular session, training to become practical theologians, and this lecture had a practical outcome. Instructed to stand up and shake off our malaise, we were asked to circulate around the classroom and position ourselves on a timeline in an attempt to locate the time that we first recognized being called to God's service. We gradually worked out our place alongside one another, those nearest to the door representing the ones who felt called early on in their lives, those furthest away representing those that felt they had recognized God's calling more recently. In this way, the time continuum became a human pathway into vocation, providing a visually powerful demonstration of the diverse nature of calling.

The exercise prompted a good deal of debate and discussion. Individual stories emerged, emphasizing the unique nature of each and every pilgrimage. We sensed that the calling of God is never uniform; that calling is a precious sign of God's infinite art; that kingdom building requires a diversity of people, ages, cultures and, of course, vocations. When we understand this, we understand that God's desire for his people can be caught by the young as well as the not so young, by explorers as well as believers.

A short time after this exercise I was ordained deacon and, a year after that, priest. The words used by the bishop to introduce the liturgy of ordination emphasize the privilege that we share in answering God's call, the privilege and the responsibility. The rite of ordination and the sacrament of Holy Orders are concerned with the development of human relationships, not least adult–child relationships which are a core concern for the Church today. The nurture of vocation and sacred identity in the broadest sense belongs to the provision of pastoral care and the cure of souls:

> Priests are called to be servants and shepherds among the people to whom they are sent ... They are to be messengers, watchmen and stewards of the Lord; they are to teach and to admonish, to feed and provide for his family, to search for his children in the wilderness of this world's temptations, and to guide them through its confusions, that they may be saved through Christ for ever.[2]
>
> (CW)

The rite of ordination provides the vocational direction for any ministry which is child or youth-focused, pointing towards the care of the Lord's family and the search for his children.[3] The rite can therefore be used as a map, a way of orientating ourselves to the borderlands of childhood where the 'messengers, watchmen and stewards of the Lord' help the young find their own way.

But what might this calling be for our children? At the very heart of this search for meaning and purpose, of identity and responsibility, God journeys with his children, his interest never wanes. Vocation is a journey of surprises and challenges, one that causes personal discomfort, but ultimately a journey that leads to communion with oneself, with the world and with God. It is the process of vocation, the journey, which I will now explore. The path to ordination and the office of Holy Orders in the Church is at times concomitant with the rocky path that many teenagers walk. As the vista of life unfolds through a new sense of independence, rationality and reason, it is not unusual for young people to find that they are under-resourced and bewildered by the world's ambivalences and dilemmas. Such disorientation is the seedbed of vocation, the probing, questioning and repositioning of the self until a place is reached which feels real, full and integrated. Many who walk this path to ordination will speak of their own feeling of perplexity, especially in terms of 'the meaning and relevance of ordination for the contemporary Church and society' (Ramsey, 1972, p. 5).

As chaplain of a boys' school, I have been privileged to a varied perspective of the young person's sacred journey. I have made my observations in chapel, on the games field, in the dining hall, in the corridors and classrooms. This daily contact with eleven to eighteen-year-olds, including girls from the sixth form, has given me a holistic viewpoint of the tensions of adolescence, its hopes and dreams, its complexities and contradictions. The school environment has allowed me to reflect upon these adolescent years in terms of education, church and faith, family and friendship groups and how all of these institutions can attract and repel the young person growing up in twenty-first-century Britain. The world of faith and belief does not escape the adolescent's sense of order and justice. Nor is the authority of God, the Church and the Bible exempt from student revolution. Here the young are battling to gain sense of truth and meaning, perhaps lacking nuance or subtlety, but nevertheless jockeying for position in order to start the adult journey. Rebecca Nye describes this adolescent tension in her essay 'Childhood and Adolescence': 'They become aware of being "at the edge" in terms of knowledge, power, adulthood, and of physical and sexual maturity. This can have implications for their faith, their spirituality, and their perception of the church' (2001a, p. 98). The adolescent search for truth and meaning comes into conflict with the holders of power and authority, be they adults or the Church. This is a borderland experience, one that brings the created world into a sharper focus for the young person.

Shoah

There is an ancient forest myth which is located primarily in the Teutonic world. Throughout history writers have referred to the wildwood and its dark properties. Over time this myth has gathered folklore status so that the forest has been the subject of many children's and adults' stories from the Brothers Grimm to Arthurian legend, Shakespeare's comedies and Hardy's Dorchester. Playwrights and novelists have shared this attraction to the wildwood, which Carl Jung uses as a nature metaphor or archetype for the collective unconscious:

It is no accident that in the comedies of Shakespeare, people go into the greenwood to grow, learn and change. It is where you travel to find yourself, often, paradoxically, by getting lost. Merlin sends the future King Arthur as a boy into the greenwood to fend for himself in *The Sword in the Stone*. There, he falls asleep and dreams himself, like a chameleon, into the lives of the animals and the trees.

(Deakin, 2008, p. ix)

When Monmouth School Chapel was given the opportunity to purchase the painting *Shoah*, which takes the wildwood as its subject, the response to the piece was divided and inspired a great deal of debate. The Hebrew word *Shoah* is enscribed upon the bottom left corner of the painting meaning calamity, disaster, desolation and catastrophe. The predominantly black and white image uses acrylic and paper as its main media. The painting takes the viewer into its heart by the way of a path engulfed by the imposing nuisance of tall, dark trees.[4]

The painting illustrates the lived-out history that woods are places where awful events take place. For the wildwoods, the darkest forests are uninhabited places where the physical nature of place strips people of their identity. *Shoah* is a powerful painting which reminds the viewer of his susceptibility to err, to fall, to cause calamity, disaster, desolation and catastrophe. In other words, the painting demonstrates the close proximity between aspects of the human condition which are life-giving and the contrary forces which seek death. These are human experiences but experiences which are felt most pressingly by the adolescent soul. The painting provokes a strong response because it was crafted from a continuing echo of terror and the loss of identity.

There is an aspect of *Shoah* which penetrates both mind and spirit. Dissecting the wildwoods, a forest track leads the eye into the 'heart of darkness'.[5] The young person's journey is one of precarious orientation, of exploration, leaving the forest track, getting lost, and, at times, losing a sense of self. Further still, the purpose of exploration is discovery – and in our case, self-discovery. The painting's purpose is to invite the searching soul to come to a kind of resolution despite the competing tensions contained within its frame. Like any young person struggling to make sense of the world, *Shoah* asks of its audience, where does the balance lie? For what we see and experience here is a dichotomy of disturbance and stillness, between that which is destructive and of death and that which is positive and creative. Laurence Freeman recently commented upon this same conflict between good and the 'self-destructiveness of evil': 'These dark forces that separate us from the holy and good spend themselves at the entrance to the very place they came to destroy.'[6] It is at these entrance places, these transition points or borderlands, especially those between adolescence and adulthood, that this conflict seems to be at its most intense.

Ordination, like the wildwood, is also a transition point which provokes a crisis of identity for all who tread its path. Religious vocation including all who aspire to serve Christ and humanity is located outside the places of comfort and safety. This, like the borderland imagery we have widely used, is a place on the edge of a known world; an outside place, one marked by contradiction, it is also a refuge where the soul may aspire to 'grow, learn and change' (Deakin, 2008). I suggest that the wildwood might also allude to the place of contrition and repentance, necessary stations on the road to vocation. *Shoah* is a painting of strong contrasts between good and evil, light and dark, growth and stagnation. Vocation, and particularly ordination, is a calling to transform the contrasts and divisions of this world which cause such pain. All those called by God are asked to 'reconcile what is divided, heal what is wounded and restore what is lost' (CW).[7] This is the work of transforming mind and spirit, a task which is central to any vocation. Transformation is the continuing narrative within the Christian story which is founded upon Jesus' resurrection, the outpouring of life for the world. This is not a story that ends in calamity or disaster. Good Friday is not the final *Shoah*-like event in the vocation of God's people. God continues to reach out and recognize the goodness of his creation. The movement from the claustrophobia of the wildwood to the infinite possibility that is creation is the hope of Easter which, as baptized adults, we are called to pass on to our children. In doing so, both wounds and divisions might be integrated with a reconciling love that the Gospel presents. Vocation is the path that leads the child into adulthood, to a place of integration within the sacred world.

Via Dolorosa

I once asked a small group of children, 'What does the word "called" mean?' Two responses stood out in particular: 'It means you are in trouble' and 'It means being asked to do something.' On reflection, both responses have real validity. While the first suggests that calling is something that involves either a threat or danger, the second suggests participation. In combination, these responses seem to highlight a truth: that God's calling leaves us both fearful and expectant. These emotions are common both to the young person's experience and to those who respond to the calling of God. The painting of *Shoah* facilitates danger and participation. It impresses the onlooker about the nature of the relationship of those who are prepared to cross the borderlands together in fear and expectation.

Young people might recognize a whole spectrum of these *Shoah*-like experiences within their own internal worlds: of losing a sense of identity or, alternately, crudely attempting to gain other identities. The compulsion to explore this wood can all too easily be attributed to adolescent angst, a significant but normative part of growing up. The wildwood represents aspects of our interior world, a world in which our spiritual and emotional health is tested. In my task as priest, and especially in my current role as school chaplain, these *Shoah* experiences remind me of my duty of care as priest, of my original calling: 'to search for [God's] children in the wilderness of this world's temptations, and to guide them through its confusions, that they may be saved through Christ for ever' (CW).[8]

The path to ordination can also be a time spent in unknowing, where the individual struggles to find a secure emotional identity, a sense of spiritual or psychological belonging. So too with adolescence. The individual perceives the world in which his core personhood is put on trial. This worldview is analogous to the way of the cross and Christ's passion. For me, the passion narrative is the path depicted in the *Shoah* painting, a path that has the potential to be immersed in both pain and sorrow, joy and thanksgiving. The depths of the human condition are to be experienced here. These are the conscious signs of a vocational journey, a primitive sense of desire to experience the height and depth of the world's joy and pain, of knowing that this can become a shared journey with Christ into the wildwood, a young person's *Via Dolorosa*. These vocational pangs and urges are formative but certainly not conclusive. All the same, the passion narrative and, in a wider frame, the whole Easter cycle, have the potential to facilitate a greater truth that an individual is known and called.

It is the seeking out of our own God-given gifts, a task that requires wisdom and discernment, that is the clue to a mature understanding of personhood and one's vocation to God. In the process of understanding our uniqueness, we might also paradoxically understand our common calling. This is a calling that involves sacrifice as well as joy. Might this be the way of the cross? Jesus knew that he embodied 'the glory of God, the pain of the world and the renewal (repentance) of the Church' (Pritchard, 2007, p. x). This calling can take a multitude of directions – many young people explore a whole range of possible career options. The process of exploration is part of what it is to be an adolescent. The important thing is that this exploration is authentic to the young person. In this sense, the adolescent's vocational path is no different from that of the adult's, lay or ordained: 'What matters is that our response to God is our response, not one determined by others, for only then shall we do best for the whole community those things that best express our own gifts'.[9]

God's calling is something akin to an Easter experience. Michael Ramsay, at what must have been an extraordinary ordination retreat, spoke pastorally and passionately to his retreatants, not only about the way of the cross, the *Via Dolorosa*, but also about the glory of the cross, Easter:

> In your service of others you will feel, you will care, you will be hurt, you will have your heart broken. And it is doubtful if any of us can do anything at all until we have been very much hurt, and until our hearts have been very much broken. And this is because God's gift to us is the glory of Christ crucified – being sensitive to the pain and sorrow that exists in so much of the world.
>
> (Cited by Sadgrove, 2008, pp. 113–114)

The way of the cross, the pilgrimage of vocation, is about identifying the places of brokenness in the world and understanding where our own gifts might be used by God to bring about healing and peace. This is what Michael Sadgrove, among others, describes as 'bearing witness'. *Shoah* is a painting that bears witness to the pain of living. 'Bearing witness' carries the sense of taking a public stance by testifying to what we have seen and heard. 'There is a story to be told, and it matters to the suffering, to the dead and to God that it should be heard' (Sadgrove, 2008, p. 112). So it is with the young that they too have stories to tell, burdens to release and hopes to explore. It is essential that adults identify with the brokenness of innocence and bear witness to its repair.

The *Via Dolorosa* might not lead to a religious vocation, but the stations of that journey might well inform and instruct us about the sacredness of life, in particular the lives of those we are called to nurture, which in this context means the young. If we are able to bear witness to the Easter story, of passion, death and resurrection, we are better equipped to discern the stories of the young and their own unique passion cycles which, when considered metaphorically, can be translated as individual narratives of trial, crisis and recovery. The role of parent, guide, teacher or priest is, therefore, vital in bearing witness, in recognizing the way of the cross and all that the pilgrimage of life represents. The passion narrative, the building block of vocation, resonates with the rite of ordination. As the newly ordained are sent out of the Mother Church by their bishop, this is their command: 'Set your heart to the promises of God; bear witness to his love for all the world' (CW). Bearing true witness to our young requires us as adults to embrace Jesus' passion, to seek out our own *Via Dolorosa* and eventually arrive at the Easter tomb.

Idols and icons

For the multitude of those involved in the vocation of the young, love's redeeming work can seem to be an impossible task. Contrition and redemption are not theological themes that sit comfortably with modern society. However, it is the business of vocation that we must at some stage in our development recognize those aspects of our lives, and the lives of those we care for, which deny life and battle against hope, growth and transformation. Many young people are consumed by distraction and diversion. Their path towards adulthood is obstructed by idols, false gods, which can claim their identity and formation. So here we are reminded of the first commandment of the Mosaic Law: 'I am the Lord your God, who brought you out of the land of Egypt, out of the house of slavery, you shall have no other gods before me.'[10]

In the untidy mix of contemporary society, the power of consumerism has merged idols into icons and icons into idols. The cult of personality has grown in an age when an aspiration of growing up is to become famous, not quite caring where that fame might come from or where it might lead (Jamison, 2008). 'Big Brother', 'The X Factor' and 'Britain's Got Talent' are powerful examples of how individualism is being promoted through hero worship. The problem here is about discernment: what tools, what resources are available for our young people to distinguish between that which is iconic and that which is idolatrous? In the Judaeo-Christian tradition, the place of 'heroes' is founded on individuals' behaviour before God and their relationship to others. The Bible presents impressive stories of individuals but always within the context of community life. These individuals have been appropriated special status such as patriarch, prophet, saint, evangelist and martyr. Through the lives of these religious superheroes the Christian narrative has an important criterion for separating idols from icons. Those who lead people towards God are, by definition, iconic. The Church today might reflect that ordination is a rite which affirms people as representatives of Christ. This is, in today's parlance, an 'iconic' rite. Church and society have a duty of care to ensure that our young people are resourced to discern between idols and icons, between that which leads to self-centredness and that which leads to a Christ-centredness. A sense of vocation in childhood and adolescence will prove to have little worth if the curiosity of our young people is limited to worshipping idols of this world's making.

Young people today in particular need role models to provide direction in a confusing moral maze. In the context of Christian vocation, the ordained members of Christ's Church may hopefully provide such direction. John Pritchard, writing about the life and work of the priest and as a former diocesan youth worker, describes the conundrum that many young people face:

> What ultimately convinces people of the value of faith is when they see it at work in someone's life. Rarely does a set of intellectual answers bring someone to faith. But when young people encounter a priest or another Christian living their faith with integrity, courage and obvious enjoyment, a process is started which opens up the possibility of a different interpretation of life which might eventually be a route to faith.
>
> (Pritchard, 2007, p. 43)

Here we have an example of where those who are on their vocational journey may help others to start their own. This is the Christian imperative that all people called to God's vocation through grace may help others in their calling. In this respect, ordination represents the granting of spiritual authority to the representatives of Christ on earth. The ordained and all those advancing on their vocational quest are the icons, the images, the windows into God's likeness.

*   *   *

The Christian narrative provided important subject matter for Western art up until the end of the seventeenth century. Used for devotional purposes, art has also served as a powerful educational tool for those seeking to learn more about this religious tradition.[11] Art is celebrated in the sacred spaces of churches and chapels in order that worshippers and visitors might be encouraged to see the world through a sacred eye. Certainly this is my hope for those who populate the school chapel: to promote a sense of critical awareness of the signs, symbols and icons within that particular sacred space.

The story of vocation and love's redeeming work is most wonderfully brought to life in a Russian icon of the fifteenth century of the descent of Christ into hell (from Novgorod). It portrays the victorious Christ in the gloom of Hades surrounded by patriarchs, kings, prophets and saints. In the foreground Jesus reaches out to two characters on bended knee – Adam and Eve. According to Irenaeus, these two adult figures were created as children, which in turn likens them to their creator. The children were then misled and tempted away from their divine likeness. This interpretation of the Fall questions whether these children were in fact responsible for their actions in the Garden. The icon describes redemption history in an instant. Adam and Eve are rescued from hell and all that this implies of being lost, alone, purposeless, without concern or care. Jesus, the Son and Saviour, restores them to life, he returns them to God the Father's intended way. They are liberated and represent redemption for all humanity. Adam and Eve in this harrowing of hell are like mythical figures which represent the children of God. Their story presents a witness to hope and transformation, which is the bedrock of our Easter faith. Their calling is to live in the image of God, in the world that God intended. They lost their way, but Christ is literally at hand even when redemption seems beyond possibility. We all need to understand our closeness to Adam and Eve, that their human condition is ours too, our own adolescent selves. God's overarching plan for his people, his design for life, is for his creation to be transformed evermore into his likeness. Perhaps young people may find succour in this narrative of liberation. Young people may seem at times unable to consider the consequences of their actions and behaviour. Yet God seeks out the lost, and helps recover our lost inheritance. For those on a vocational journey, the calling is clear: if we as adults are to liberate the harrowed places which open up the way to vocation, we must, where necessary, seek out God's children and, as co-workers in Christ, offer them a hand.

Sabbath and sanctuary

St Augustine of Hippo, writing at the end of the fourth century, declared, 'Because God has made us for Himself, our hearts are restless until they rest in Him.' The statement could describe both the path leading to ordination and the experience of adolescence. This restlessness is displayed through significant traits of understanding and behaviour. The boys that are in my care are constantly wanting, needing to prove, test, taste and judge all that is offered to them. Theirs is a borderland experience as they stand restlessly on the threshold of an adult world in need of reforming and reshaping.

Young people need time to rest, as Augustine states. Yet rest in modern culture is deemed to be less attractive. The Christian alternative to a seven-day week is, of course, a six-day week, the seventh being a day of recreation, of refreshment, of rest. This Sabbath day ultimately provides a structure, a discipline, a rule of life. In the complex process of growing up, the Sabbath gives order. This is sacred time which provides space to do less rather than more. During breaks between lessons, before school and after school, mobile phones and iPods are at the ready. When time allows, the super highway provides a conduit for a myriad of digital adventures. Bebo and Facebook are essential modes of communication, of connecting to the wider social world. For the iPod generation, time is an opportunity to fill rather than to empty.

The Genesis story presents creation with an order, a process. Crossing the borderlands of childhood requires time as well as order. Through the process of identity, formation and vocation, time has been committed to the glory of God, the purpose of the Sabbath. By crossing the borderlands, priority has been given to God's time and not our own. Restless though we are, the Sabbath has been given as a necessary gift, to reflect and give thanks for our journey. Sabbath is the day of resurrection, Easter Day. Every Sunday, Christians celebrate the greatest of all miracles, the empty tomb. It is a day like no other. In this context, Sabbath is therefore a gift that we also can pass on to our children.

Adolescents need their own space as well as time; physical space which provides grounds for their search for meaning and truth. In *Finding Sanctuary: Monastic Steps for Everyday Life*, Christopher Jamison observes:

> Sanctuary has two meanings: the primary meaning comes from the Latin root word, *sanctus,* meaning 'holy.' So the first meaning is 'a sacred space,' and deriving from this comes the secondary meaning: 'a place of refuge,' a place where someone on the run can escape to.
> (Jamison, 2006, p. 22)

For many young people, the sacred space of sanctuary can be challenging. The function of a church or chapel is to provide an environment for prayer and praise, both individual and corporate. Monmouth School Chapel is almost exclusively used for corporate worship in the form of house chapel services which require hymn singing and occasionally the recitation of psalms. The elements within any given liturgy requiring a corporate response demand an empathetic, listening ear. The singing of hymns or recitation of psalms should be a unified response, as one body. For many of the students this is quite foreign, a counter-cultural experience which highlights the extent to which individualistic expression holds sway. As the students file into chapel they, like so many of their peers, struggle to keep silence. Their head noise continues as their amplified voices fill the sacred space. They find silence difficult to tolerate, they have not been given the art of stillness[12] or silence. The culture which to a large extent has formed them does not acknowledge silence as a common good, rather the contrary. The 'still small voice' of God is drowned. How can silence and stillness be inculcated into the lives of the young? For the silence of sanctuary within them needs to be nurtured and cared for.

The creation of a sanctuary, of a sacred person or place, requires the community to make it holy; it is sacred as a result of the people who create its silence, stillness and space. If a place of sanctuary is to be present in the borderlands of adolescence, time and space needs to be invested in the lives of our young people. This returns us to sanctuary's secondary meaning, that of a refuge, a safe place where resolution and reconciliation may be explored or even found. This definition seems even more apposite in the context of nurturing vocation. It is not only the young who need to find out who they are and become reconciled to themselves, to their world and to God if their vocational search is to be a fruitful search. As adults seeking to nurture the young, we too need to find ways of offering sanctuary, remembering also that, before we can offer sanctuary, we need to find it (Jamison, 2006).

The vocation of a priest, following the example of Jesus, is to open up sanctuary, to open the doors of faith and possibility. This is the vocation that both Church and society need to encourage. The constant challenge of such a vocation is to keep time as God's time. The Sabbath provides sacred time and space to hear God's calling. In the context of the child, the calling of creation is a calling to become icons – bearers of God's likeness through the image of Christ. The kingdom of God, glimpsed through the borderlands of childhood, is where we recognize God's image fully. The kingdom is the place where we as adults recognize that our children, born in the image of God, called by the Spirit, become the icons of Christ.

Chapter 8

Adolescence

Troubled territory

While adolescence has its first, formal roots in the early twentieth century, Greek philosophers such as Aristotle and Plato were writing about the difficulties experienced by youngsters during puberty more than two thousand years ago.[1] The borderlands of adolescence have, it seems, long since been marked out as troubled territory. This is the place where one's identity is sought;[2] where voices are explored and fought over; where a sense of belonging, particularly to one's peer group, is crucial but by no means guaranteed; and where battles lost and tears shed have a multitude of consequences.

Today's media offer constant reminders of where our young are going wrong. The increase of knife and gun crime in the UK, of youth against youth, and of several high-profile cases in recent years, have generated a very real concern about the pressures on modern youth, about the breakdown of traditional values and homes, and perhaps even a loss of identity for those whose identity is key to the future. In this context, an age-old stereotype is being reinforced in which adolescence is increasingly associated with disturbance, characterized by crime, violence, sex, drugs and alcohol.[3]

This stereotype needs, however, to be set against a strong word of caution. The fact remains that a problem-saturated youth is 'neither inevitable nor normative' (Adams and Berzonsky, 2003). Empirical research over the past two decades has demonstrated that, despite the difficulties associated with this period, the majority of adolescents in fact achieve a path into adulthood which bodes well for the future (Adams and Berzonsky, 2003). From our perspective, this path is best rooted in spiritual turf, in an adolescent's emerging sense of vocation. In order to consider what this might mean in practical terms, I shall begin with Gavin's definition of ordination:

> The call to ordination represents a disciplined commitment to serve the people of God alongside Christ. To be ordained, then, is to live according to God's holy law; to understand that the world in which we are situated is sacred, it is of God.

Ideas of 'disciplined commitment' and living 'according to God's holy law' do not exactly equate with fashionable speak. The call to commitment does, though, remind me of the tenor of the Good Childhood Inquiry, and the specific recommendation first cited in the introduction, that parents make a long-term commitment to one another. A key theme of ordination (commitment) clearly does not start and end with a calling to the priesthood. The language of commitment to God and to each other is one that might usefully be applied to us all. Commitment involves both stability and continuity regardless of the way ahead. It is a quality which an adolescent needs both to experience first-hand and be able to emulate if he is to find out what vocation means for him in the broadest sense. It is, therefore, through a willingness to commit, not only to one another but to our young, and ultimately to God, that we enable an adolescent to find his own way across the borderlands. In this chapter, I shall consider how a vocational framework, as already explored through the rite of ordination, might further enrich a psychological understanding of adolescence.

The Diary of Anne Frank

At the start of my second year at secondary school, when I was not quite thirteen, our English teacher presented us with our new book for the term: *The Diary of Anne Frank*. This diary, written by a Jewish girl in her early teens in occupied Holland during the Second World War has, for over sixty years, captured the hearts and minds of people across all nations and all ages. Translated into 66 languages, it has been adapted for television, radio and stage. The 'secret annexe' in Amsterdam where Anne, her family and others were hidden has been open to the public since 1960, and exhibitions and related conferences continue to be held world-wide. While efforts were initially made to brand the diary a fake, these accusations have long since been disproved. Anne, along with the rest of the annexe household, was taken from hiding in August 1944; she subsequently died in the concentration camp in Bergen-Belsen from typhus, just a few days after her sister Margot.

I started to read *Anne Frank* on my journey home from school. That night, I read late into the night and finished reading it. Our homework for English that week: to start a diary. It was suggested that we could call our diary a name. I chose 'Anne'. Anne would, as it happened, become my companion and confidante for the remainder of my adolescence. To her I would speak, without apology, of all things. My entries would be rambling, giving no thought to editorship. Details of anything and everything were captured there: misdemeanours, misunderstandings, broken friendships, unrequited loves, family arguments, painstaking efforts to observe and describe my world as I perceived it, internal and external. In time, however, the entries waned and, when perhaps at last I was starting to see a little outside myself, the diary stopped altogether.

I was not the first, and certainly shall not be the last, adolescent girl to have been affected by the life and story of Anne Frank. Her story of robbed identity, of loss, of suffering and ultimately of death will undoubtedly affect generations to come. And yet, though it was written within the context of horrifying and oppressive circumstances, the preoccupations of the diary itself are remarkably familiar. In Anne's descriptions of daily living, factors common to any adolescent are digested and exposed at different levels: what it means to feel on the outside, to experience fractured relationships, to come to terms with physical changes associated with puberty, to struggle to relate to those around oneself, to long for some kind of transformation, a return to normality when all is well again. As in my own adolescence I entered Anne's world, while I understood that my context was utterly different, that her challenges were challenges I could not begin to imagine, I found I could relate to her introspections, her private yearnings, her internal and external conflicts. This sense of relationship to Anne is of course one of the touchstones of the diary:

Anne was first and foremost a teenage girl, not a remote and flawless symbol. She fretted about, and tried to cope with, her emerging sexuality. Like many young girls, she often found herself in disagreement with her mother. And, like any teenager, she veered between the carefree nature of a child and the fully fledged sorrow of an adult.[4]

Anne's trials and labours are evocative, therefore, of tensions common to many adolescents: deep introspection, on the one hand; a desire to think outside oneself, to contemplate a better world, on the other. 'Society', wrote Winnicott, 'needs to be shaken by the aspirations of those who are not responsible [i.e. adolescents]' (1971/1991, p. 146). Anne's own aspirations, which she voices increasingly throughout her diary, underpinned by her unique and tragic circumstances, articulate a deep recognition of the human susceptibility to err, but articulate also an aspiration to keep faith in human capacity for goodness despite this. In one of her last diary entries before being captured, she wrote:

It's a wonder I haven't abandoned all my ideals, they seem so absurd and impractical. Yet I cling to them because I still believe, in spite of everything, that people are truly good at heart.

It's utterly impossible for me to build my life on a foundation of chaos, suffering and death. I see the world being slowly transformed into a wilderness … And yet, when I look up at the sky …I must hold on to my ideals.

(*Diary of Anne Frank*, Saturday 15 July 1944)

Anne's 'ideals' (or 'aspirations', to use Winnicott's phrase) are born out of a direct *Shoah* experience, in which she must somehow seek to separate light from dark, good from evil. Her poignant and ever-real attempts to do this are repeatedly characterized by her faith:

People who are religious should be glad, since … religion itself, any religion, keeps a person on the right path. How noble and good everyone could be if, at the end of each day, they were to review their own behaviour and weigh up the rights and wrongs.

(*Diary of Anne Frank*, Thursday 6 July 1944)

For my part, Anne's writing, painful and disturbing, gave me a timely insight into what it means to consider one's own actions and the actions of others. These first insights are, it seems, central to an adolescent's path. Torn between looking in and looking out, the experiences need to be internalized in order for an adolescent, at least in time, to grow up and see beyond the borders of his immediate ken, even to understand something of his vocational calling.

'When were you called by God?' The question might startle your average adolescent – certainly it would have terrified me – but, with hindsight, I think perhaps I would want to return to my adolescence when seeking to answer it. I would not know of course what God was calling me to (I still do not know that), but I do know where on that timeline I would want to stand. I would place myself firmly on the section marked 'aged thirteen'. I would even perhaps be tempted to embellish it further, scribing with my own hand, 'First day of a new term, second year, senior school. The day I read *Anne Frank.*' To enter another's world at a significant stage in one's own emotional development, to stop and consider what it might be like to be another, to suffer alongside and to hold in mind, this experience is deeply vocational. Perhaps it also speaks of something of what Winnicott had in mind when he described an adolescent's aspirations: 'creative thought, new and fresh feeling, ideas for new living' (Winnicott, 1971/1991, p. 146). These aspirations are borderland in nature and might well be met with painful consequences. In seeking to realize his aspirations, the adolescent will, in the words of Michael Ramsey, almost certainly 'feel ... care ... be hurt ... have [his] heart broken'.[5] Through this process, if encouraged and nurtured, he will move closer to finding out not only his identity but also his vocation.

Identity and vocation

The concept of vocation in a religious sense has little or no place in the psychological literature on adolescence. Unsurprisingly, however, its secular counterparts (work, career and occupation) most certainly do. For half a century now, there has existed a strong connection between the theme of identity and work. 'In general,' Erikson wrote, 'it is primarily the inability to settle on an occupational identity which disturbs young people' (1950/1995, p. 97). Erikson's thesis has been well endorsed and elaborated by psychologists since (e.g. Vondracek and Porfeli, 2003; Carr, 2006). Adolescence is, after all, the stepping-stone to the adult world and a key task of the adult world, whether 'high achieving' or 'non-achieving', 'happy' or 'unhappy', is work.

Because of the tragic way in which Anne Frank's life was cut short, her identity and vocation were never fully realized. And yet through her writing she demonstrates in both mind and spirit a unique ability to engage and empathize with others. Though she was just fifteen when she died, her strong sense of self and identity were already rooted in a desire to work and to serve others, which was part of her burgeoning religious belief:

> We have many reasons to hope for great happiness, but ... we have to earn it. And that's something you can't achieve by taking the easy way out. Earning happiness means doing good and working, not speculating and being lazy. Laziness may *look* inviting, but only work gives you *true* satisfaction.
>
> (*Diary of Anne Frank*, Thursday 6 July 1944)

Interestingly, Anne goes on to equate a commitment to work with both a belief in one's abilities and a belief in God. In this way, Anne's diary is a powerful witness to what it is to feel called. Her own thoughts on work have much in common with Frederick Buechner's definition of vocation: 'True vocation joins self and service; it comes from the place where your deep gladness meets the world's deep need' (Buechner, 1973, p. 119).[6]

When considering here the vast spectrum of today's young, it seems important to emphasize that work and vocation might include any number of callings, gifts and strengths, and are certainly not confined to a limited definition of what work or a calling might be. The underlying point is that the young person needs time and space to work out for themselves the beliefs and values they hold close to them. This is central to one type of identity formation, what Erikson calls 'moratorium' (1950/1995): 'Where adolescents achieve a clear identity following a successful moratorium, they develop a strong commitment to vocational, social, political and religious values and usually have good psychosocial adjustment in adulthood' (Carr, 2006, p. 31). In this interpretation of moratorium, it seems that ideas of vocation and religion have crept in almost after the event, that is once an individual's identity and his ability to settle on work has been achieved. But perhaps this is not as back-to-front as it seems. Vocation is, after all, frequently a process of misturnings and reorientations before one's path is found. The important thing is that the adolescent is encouraged to explore and experiment with this vocational process. 'Sabbath and sanctuary' are essential ingredients here: that is, time out to consider and reflect, not just time filled up with activity and distraction.

As adults concerned for today's young, we have a responsibility to facilitate young people's identity formation, to enable their path to 'a successful moratorium'. The space for discussion, at home, at school, in any community setting, all offer opportunity for this. This is one of the huge strengths of the Taizé community as, in its vocation to call the young, it encourages not only space and silence but the daily opportunity to come together in small groups and reflect on biblical passages, to ask questions and explore. The importance of these kinds of opportunities cannot be underestimated as they allow young people to ask questions about who they are, 'not just in the context of other people but of life's greater meaning and their reason for being' (Ream and Savin-Williams, 2003, p. 53). As adults, however, with strongly held beliefs of our own, we need to be cautious about pushing our own agenda; to remember first and foremost 'that the relationships of young people with the divine are their own, and as individual as the young themselves' (Ream and Savin-Williams, p. 57). Where the growth of a young person's psychosocial identity is integrated with his relationship to God, the potential for a lasting moratorium is achieved.

But this process cannot and must not take place quickly. As adolescents explore who they are and who they would like to be, they are likely to experiment with a variety of roles, to pit themselves against those adults that mean most to them, exchanging former role models for new ones (Erikson, 1950/1995, p. 235). From a psychoanalytical perspective, difficult feelings are not tolerated by the adolescent and are instead projected onto another 'object', what Margot Waddell (1998) defines as 'the scapegoat', such as the parent or teacher. This process, known as projective identification, allows the adolescent to disown his own feelings and so exist in an 'out-of-touch-with-oneself' state which is preferable to the underlying sense of fear and bewilderment. This is, according to Waddell, a wilderness state, 'a rough and desolate area where the individual wanders and loses his/her way ... both sought and feared by this age group.' (Waddell, p. 135).

There is something deeply vocational about this wandering. A fine line is struck between keeping the adolescent safe and allowing him to find out for himself his own route, his own journey. 'The ministry of the good Shepherd wasn't just to keep the flock safe; it was to guide them to a new pasture' (Pritchard, 2007, p. 69). In both theological and psychoanalytical terms, therefore, the wilderness of adolescence has much in common with the *Shoah* experience. In the painting *Shoah*, the wildwood is the place where individuals have been unable to tolerate their own feelings, to tolerate difference in others; where the 'object' has been scapegoated and thereby victimized. Adolescents who journey through this wildwood without losing themselves completely will find ways of tolerating these feelings of difference and confusion. Rupture with the 'good object', be this a parent figure, a teacher or the Church, will only be transitory and an important part of growing up, enabling the young person to emerge from the wildwood with his identity in tact.

A vocation in waiting

As adolescents seek out and struggle with their *Shoah* experiences, it is almost inevitable that families can come under a great deal of pressure. And yet, this period of procrastination, of getting it wrong and starting again, is in fact central to the task of adolescence. 'When were you called by God?' This is not a question that can, by definition, be asked until after the event. Nor, however, is it a question that should ever stagnate, that should leave an individual feeling that they have arrived in a comfortable place, that somehow they can now stop looking. The vocational journey, though clearly marked by critical points in one's life, has no fixed end but is founded on the task of waiting: 'For anyone who has stopped waiting, anyone who has settled down in himself, his privileges or his rights, a whole dimension of faith has shrivelled away' (Brother Roger of Taizé, 1981, p. 67). The ability to wait, to resist settling down in oneself, has much in common with the task of adolescence. For adolescence, which spans several years and plays host to a whole complex of changes – physical, hormonal, social, emotional and cognitive[7] – is not a task that should be rushed.

If an adolescent's calling is to be nurtured in any meaningful sense, then the period of adolescence is, above all, about waiting. A very real and contemporary concern is that, as the pace of life constantly gathers momentum, childhood and, by the same token, adolescence, is forever shrinking. Ground down by a modern culture of 'selfish' living, of competitive values and excessive consumerism and marketing (Layard and Dunn, 2009), the period of adolescence is in danger of becoming shorter and shorter. It is frequently said that children must be allowed to be children. Similarly, adolescents must be allowed to be adolescents. Winnicott (1971/1991) stated this unequivocally almost four decades ago, writing in *Playing and Reality*:

> Immaturity is an essential element of health at adolescence. There is only one cure for immaturity and that is the passage of time and the growth into maturity that time may bring.
> ... If the adults abdicate, the adolescent becomes prematurely, and by false process, adult. Advice to society could be: for the sake of adolescents, and of their immaturity, do not allow them to step up and attain a false maturity by handing over to them responsibility that is not yet theirs, even though they may fight for it.
>
> (Winnicott, p. 146)

Winnicott's plea to adults to be adults so that children can retain their status as children is somewhat prophetic.[8] If adolescence is not to be hurried, then adulthood must be waited for. What is more, this waiting will only come about if the adults are willing and mature enough to allow today's adolescents the immaturity of their age, to enable them to work things out for themselves, and not have a pseudo-responsibility thrust upon them. This challenge as adults, to enable and actively encourage today's young to slow down, not to race to the 'finishing line' only to discover it does not exist, is a deeply non-secular one. It defies the current tide of instant gratification, of competitiveness, consumerism, premature sexualization and lightening communication, and instead places value on that which must be anticipated, not by constantly looking ahead in an effort to glimpse round the corner, but by living in the here and now. As Paula Gooder writes: 'Antipathy to waiting is exacerbated, if not encouraged, by the world in which we live. All around us we encounter, day after day, the encouragement not to wait but to have what we want now' (2008, p. 2).

What might it mean for the adolescent to wait? To sit in the park with a friend and, instead of being focused on his mobile, texting another friend two miles away, to remain focused instead on the conversation with his friend in the park, right where he is sitting? When we cease to live in the present, we have ceased to wait and, from a faith perspective, we have forgotten the essence of our discipleship, of what it is to be in relationship with one another, and ultimately in relationship with God.

Waiting is therefore deeply vocational. It demands that we grapple with questions such as 'Where am I travelling?' and 'Where is home?' I, for one, am particularly bad at it. It would seem I would do well to learn from Winnicott's thesis of adolescence, and carry it perhaps still further; that is, to understand that, if I want to instil in my children the gift of waiting, of allowing the pattern of their lives to unfold not in their or others' time but in God's time, then I will need to take a hard look at my own natural impatience and all-too-ready sense of frustration, my impoverished prayer life and short fuse, and consider how these might be impacting not only on the dimensions of my own faith but on my relationship to others.

If we struggle with this task as adults, it seems a tall order to impose it somehow on the generations of youth that come up behind us. The point, however, is not that waiting is imposed on adolescents but rather that their core waiting experience is seen as preparation ground for a life's vocation in which a desire for instant gratification is overturned by a deeper knowledge of all that waiting can bring. Through this process both adolescent and adult might gain a living insight into what Brother Roger calls 'the dynamic of the provisional':

'To realize this means realizing as well that we are living in a state that is always provisional. Provisional has the same root as provide. Provide the measures necessary until another set of circumstances arises' (1981, p. 67).

To be reconciled to the idea of a provisional world is to understand one's temporary place within it; to reconcile oneself to an image which stands contrary to the consumerist drive of today, and which seeks to find out a different set of values, one which endorses the place where we came from and where we are journeying to. These values, central to our faith are caught and not taught. But the place in which these values are caught is a borderland place, meaning that the adolescent will have to risk growing up with values that contradict those of his peers. This is not to say that he will stand apart from his peer group altogether, far from it. But each adolescent needs to work out for himself the tension between individuality and membership of a group if he is to carve out his path to adulthood:

> The young adolescent faces a dilemma of group identity versus alienation. There is a requirement to find a peer group with which to become affiliated so that the need for belonging will be met. Joining such a group, however, must not lead to sacrificing one's individuality and personal goals and aspirations. If young adolescents are not accepted by a peer group they will experience alienation.
>
> (Carr, 2006, p. 30)

Underpinning this dilemma of adolescence is, therefore, a profoundly vocational task: namely, that God calls his children into relationship with one another, to live not separately but as communities while understanding that, within these communities, their individuality is marked.

Letting go

The adolescent treads a fine line between working out his own individuality and his sense of belonging in a group. This occurs in the familial as well as the peer setting. At home, the challenge for parents is to enable their adolescent to achieve a balance between individuality and 'group identity' (Graham, 1998). This balance can be hard to achieve, particularly where parents struggle to allow their adolescent to adopt the position of 'outsider', a position which is thought to be essential to their overall development (Dartington, 1994, cited by Graham, 1998, p. 146). This 'outside' position can be deeply painful for parents, particularly where parent–child bonds are close-knit and the status quo seems threatened. And yet, if adolescents are not given this 'outside' space, this permission to live on the edge of the group (while understanding still that they remain integral to it), they will not be given the space to understand for themselves who they want to be.

This is a task and challenge not only for parents. It is also a task for the Church. Recent literature on adolescents' place in the Church has frequently focused on efforts to encourage the young to remain within the body of the Church during their adolescent years, or to recruit them into it, and so provide them with a sense of belonging (e.g. Ream and Savin-Williams, 2003). The merits of this argument are self-evident. But the Church, like parents, needs also to know how to let go of its young when necessary; to understand that, if adolescents are to work out their own path, then they are likely to wander, to adopt an 'outside' position if they are to grow. The process inevitably leaves the Church with a dilemma. But just as parents need to tussle with holding on and letting go, of allowing adolescents to live on the edge while understanding that their place is integral, so too does the Church.

A recent 'Fresh Expressions' initiative seemed to reflect whole-hearted understanding of this dilemma: a vicar decided to open Malmesbury Abbey as a skateboard park over a bank holiday weekend. Interviewed by local and national press, the Reverend Neill Archer offered the following explanation for the initiative:

> We see the young people walk past the abbey every day and they probably think it doesn't have relevance to them, that it doesn't belong to them, that it's for the older people and the tourists. And then they believe the Christian faith doesn't belong to them, so on a number of levels we're saying, 'you're

welcome here, your culture is welcome here.' ... We are trying something that is on the edge in order to connect with young people.[9]

I happened to hear Neill Archer speaking on the radio one morning around this time. He articulated his strong belief that he had no high expectation of his initiative; he was happy for the young to remain on the outside, but he also thought that the experience would perhaps offer a different perspective – plant the seed that, while they retained an 'outsider' position to the Church, their membership of it was implicit.

It is possible that the tension between exclusion and inclusion is painful for parents and the Church alike, but this tension is necessary if adolescents are to step to one side and find out for themselves the different voices (of belief and unbelief, of belonging and not belonging, of calling and non-calling) that speak to them. Many young people will be 'lost' during this process but if they are lost freely, then perhaps they are more likely to return. Again, this might well be difficult for all involved because the process does not occur overnight, but the process is, to use Winnicott's word, 'sacred' and essential to an adolescent's health and development. As Paul Upson (1998) writes:

> Most crucial of all is the need for the individual adolescent to have time and space to work 'on' – if not precisely 'work out' – the balance between the positive/creative/life enhancing and the negative/destructive/death dealing forces inside themselves.
>
> (p. 161)

If young people are actively encouraged to seek out this time and space, they are given the opportunity to push themselves even further to that borderland place; to retain an outside position while seeking also to find home.

Living on the edge

At a symbolic level, the process of seeking time and space is a kind of *Shoah* experience: for the family as a whole, for a community, for a church and the individuals within it. In psychoanalytical terms, the process might even feel violent, a terrifying threat to all that has gone before it as, in order for the individual to mature and achieve adult status, there is, at least in the unconscious world, *'the death of someone'* (Winnicott, 1971):

> Even when the growth at the period of puberty goes ahead without major crises, one may need to deal with acute problems of management because growing up means taking the parent's place. *It really does.* In the unconscious fantasy, growing up is inherently an aggressive act.
>
> (Winnicott, 1971, p. 144)

This process can be painful for all involved. In my work, I have frequently encountered adolescents for whom this 'working out' has gone significantly wrong somewhere and the balance between the two forces, positive and negative, has been knocked off key, leaving an individual vulnerable and exposed in both mind and spirit. This can manifest itself in any number of mental health difficulties, including anxiety, depression, early signs of psychosis (e.g. schizophrenia or bipolar disorder), eating disorders, aggression and so on. During my years working in London, many of the adolescents referred to child and family teams, both within the context of special needs and mental health, were refugees. Frequently living in temporary accommodation, including hostels and bed and breakfasts, these families' status as outsiders, culturally, linguistically, socially and economically, was, almost without exception, tantamount. In this deeply troubled context, it often seemed that a parent's difficulty in enabling their adolescent to separate, to adopt that 'outside' position, almost re-enacted traumas previously experienced by the family, traumas of lost home, country, dignity, culture and even part of the family itself. This difficulty, so pronounced in many of the refugee families I have worked with, finds expression in a whole range of families struggling to cope with the 'vortex' of adolescence (Graham, 1998, p. 143), particularly where any kind of loss, instability, trauma or breakdown is present.

I have as yet no experience of parenting an adolescent myself. I do not, therefore, yet know, I can only imagine, what it might be like to live with an individual who needs to live on the edge, to reposition themselves in relation to family life and the relationships within it. When I have worked with adolescents individually in a therapeutic setting, I have frequently been aware that the process of separation can be painful, even frightening, for the parents or caregivers involved. This difficulty with separation is frequently re-enacted in the therapeutic relationship itself. What is their teenager saying to me? What am I saying back to them? Will I judge the parents, condemn them, join forces with their child against them? Or will I provide a miracle cure, absolve them of any responsibility, and replace them altogether?

Though I have only witnessed (and not yet experienced) what it can mean to parent a teenager, I cannot pretend I do not know what it means to feel on the outside of a significant relationship, to struggle with the undeniable anguish and reality of needing to separate in order to allow another to find out for themselves who they are and where they might be going. The experience for me was deeply painful. I struggled to retain my own sense of individuality within it. It was also a borderland experience, an experience in which my faith and core values were put to trial repeatedly. With hindsight, I think this experience was not only a reenactment of past hurts and unresolved patterns of relating, but also a rehearsal for the future: an opportunity to work out and reflect on what it means to be on the edge, to understand the necessary pain of enduring and surviving an experience if I am to come closer to seeking a relationship both with others and with God.

Repentance and *metanoia*

When I look back at these occasions in my life where I have felt on the outside, one period in particular, I cannot pretend that I like what I see. This is, I confess, my *Shoah* experience, the place where I came against the darker forces of my nature, my rage, my jealousy, my anger and my hurt, and projected them elsewhere, onto an object outside myself. It was through this process of projective identification that I fought, wept and denied; but from which also, at least in time I hope, I came to aspire 'to grow, to learn and to change' (Deakin, 2008).[10]

Even though the years have separated that experience from the present, to this day I am left with a feeling of wanting to find atonement, of admitting that I did wrong, I made a mistake, not once but again and again, in failing to have faith in something that existed outside myself, which I could not control, which to me threatened isolation and loss, and which I was not prepared to risk. I have grappled with this sense of regret for years. In one way, I am fortunate. There were no long-term consequences of my scape-goating, of my failure to let another go and find out for themselves who they were. And yet, as I write and those same feelings return, those feelings of regret and a desire to say 'I was wrong, I am sorry,' I realize how deeprooted these feelings are, and how closely they are linked to 'a desire to go home' (Radcliffe, 2008, p. 21). This 'desire to go home' is potentially present in us all, however quietly that desire might have slept or rebelled against its original nature, for the desire to repent and be forgiven – to run home like the prodigal son and kneel before our father – is always possible.

Repentance is, above all, about relationship. It is 'inseparably, an awakening to God, oneself and to each other' (Radcliffe, 2008, p. 21). At the heart of repentance lies the potential for *metanoia*: for conversion, for renewal and for moving on. These feelings have the ability, therefore, to awake in me a desire to take heed, to learn from my past mistakes, to understand that in the future I might be vulnerable again and that, in my own vulnerability and need, I must endeavour not to hinder my children's development, but to allow them to find their own individuality and trust that they will return. In my own sense of awakening I hope I might, at least in glimpses, be more alive to my children's needs, their identity, formation and sense of vocation.

Not all responsibility, however, remains with the parental figure. As the individual leaves adolescence behind and prepares for his onward journey, part of moving up that fragile spectrum of maturity is to find that same ability to repent, to stop and admit where one has gone wrong, to recognize not only one's parents' fallibilities but also one's own, to understand the core test of being human, of opening oneself up to God's grace and seeking discipleship in Christ. Clearly it is deeply unhelpful to make blanket statements about this type of responsibility. The individual factors of every situation and relationship, not least where abuse has taken place or where trust has broken down, make it impossible to offer a glib notion of healing. And yet, as so many who have worked in reconciliation will testify, the human capacity to turn around and start again is almost beyond imagination.

Only in the briefest moments do I begin to recognize this potential in myself, all too easily forgotten, cast aside for a prevailing whim or emotion. But despite all that I am starting to sense that the experience of parenthood is a vocational one, not simply because we are called to hold our children sacred, to nurture them in all senses, but also because to be a parent is, as with any vocational path, to be pushed to the edge of one's own limitations; to be called back from the edge when least expected; to search out anew, admit where one has gone wrong and to start afresh. This need to repent and start again is not only true for a parent but for all adults involved with today's young. What is more, it is true for the Church as a whole:

> If the decline of the Church is ultimately caused neither by the irrel-evance of Jesus, nor by the indifference of the community, but the Church's failure to respond fast enough to an evolving culture, to a changing spiritual climate, and the promptings of the Holy Spirit, then that decline can be addressed by the repentance of the Church.
>
> (*Mission-Shaped Church*, p. 14)

Adolescence is not the only place to which immaturity belongs. But as adults seeking to work with or live alongside children and the young, we have a responsibility to give up our own immaturity so that the children of today might have their share of that luxury themselves. Only by doing this will we allow today's children to seek and find a vocational path for themselves, one which will test and shape them, which will enrich their relationships to others, and ultimately to God. Immaturity will not, of course, fade with adoles-cence. The path to maturity is a lifetime's work but, with the ending of adolescence and the emergence into early adulthood, hopefully a desire will come about in which the young adult feels able to say: 'I want to want to set aside my selfish desires; I want to want to help others and seek out a calling of my own.'[11] This wanting for something outside ourselves can be a homesick feeling. To be called, therefore, and to seek to respond to that calling, is to turn oneself around and set off not to a new place altogether, somewhere of our own making, but back to that first place from where we started out, which awaits us all, and which represents our final homecoming.

Integrating Mind and Spirit (Part 4)

Vocation

Vocation is not a product that can be purchased in the market-place, but stems from a long and protracted process in which the individual seeks to understand himself in relationship to the world, to others and to God. The lengthy nature of this process is reflected in the rite of ordination when the bishop turns directly to the ordinands and says, 'We trust that long ago you began to weigh and ponder all this …' Even at this late stage, the ordinands are reminded that vocation is not something to be rushed into. It takes time, and time is sacrosanct. As adults with a responsibility for today's young, in particular adolescents, we would do well to take heed from this reminder. Adolescence, whose most precious quality is its immaturity,[1] is also not something to be rushed. And yet in modern society this critical stage of development seems in constant danger of being short-circuited through consumerist values, through adults' refusal to consider the needs of the young before their own.

The Church has a specific vocation to 'call alongside', to 'bear witness' to the young, particularly those who are situated on the edge of organized religion. At the heart of this calling is the recognition of the struggle and competing tensions and distractions of this age. The borderlands of adolescence are shaped and defined by these tensions. As the adolescents struggle to find their identity, those who care for them must be prepared to encounter both pain and sorrow, to admit their shortcomings and mistakes as the adolescent sets about making their own. From the young person's perspective, vocation develops when confusion is met with a spirit of encouragement. Through openness and transparency, of developing sacred spaces, the quest for meaning and purpose begins.

Called to respond

Calling is shaped by others. The rite of ordination is a community experience which holds Christ at the centre. When we hear the bishop's commission to the newly ordained, the Church becomes a witness to new life and growth. In reflecting upon the following passage, how might you respond personally or corporately (for example, as a family, school or church) to its calling?

The Commission within the Rite of Ordination (CW)

Through your Spirit, heavenly Father,
give these your servants grace and power
to proclaim the gospel of your salvation
and minister the sacraments of the new covenant.
Renew them in holiness,
and give them wisdom and discipline
to work faithfully with those committed to their charge.
In union with their fellow servants in Christ,
may they reconcile what is divided,
heal what is wounded
and restore what is lost.

May they declare your blessings to your people;
may they proclaim Christ's victory over the powers of darkness,
and absolve in Christ's name those who turn to him in faith;
so shall a people made whole in Christ
offer spiritual sacrifices acceptable to you,
our God and Father,
to whom, with the Son and the Holy Spirit,
belong glory and honour, worship and praise, now and for ever.
Amen

Epilogue

We had reached the end of our Big Idea pilgrimage and descended the windswept ridge that divided Wales from England. Our destination, Llanthony Priory, sat comfortably in the valley beneath. This homecoming amongst the grandeur and austerity of the Black Mountains provided a context, a sense of perspective, not only for this particular pilgrimage, but also for my vocational journey as a father and a priest. The priory in its ruined state spoke of past glory, of legends deeply rooted in a border landscape. Yet the faith that had been fostered here and throughout the Christian world is awaiting rediscovery in this new age. As I looked upon the line of pilgrims approaching their journey's end, my hope was that this generation of borderlanders might heed the danger signs which apply to contemporary culture: individualism, competitiveness, consumerism, spiritual decay, environmental crises. These are the destructive complexities of our twenty-first-century society which shape the future of childhood forever.

The borderland children have travelled a long way – at least in the frame of reference set out in this book. We, the guides, the carers, the observers, have crossed the borderlands with them. For all of us, adults and children, this has been a pilgrimage of mind and spirit. From the identification of the sacred soul at baptism we have sought to discover the formation of that same soul journeying towards God's vocation. The child has been marked by significant physical, social, emotional and cognitive transitions from infancy to middle childhood and finally to adolescence. In all of this we have ventured to make the crossing as a Church, as a family, called by God. The distinctive nature of this family's creed has been informed at each stage of the journey through the pattern of the liturgical year, in particular, Epiphany, Lent, Holy Week and Easter. These are the seasons that integrate the holy mysteries of discovery, awareness and transformation. Epiphany is the time of discovery as we seek to understand the nature of God in Jesus. Lent is the season of awareness when we are called to cross thresholds of comfort and pain in an environment that necessitates growth. Holy Week and Easter are the culmination of this liturgical cycle, bearing witness to sacred time and space which speaks of transformation. God's promise to his people is realized, God brings his people home.

From the joint perspectives of priest and psychologist, our writing has taken us into unfamiliar and at times uncomfortable territory. To our surprise, we have both been led towards a place of repentance – repentance for ourselves as well as seeking repentance for our children's generation. Time after time this word *metanoia* fills our language. *Metanoia* is the energy that is released, the commitment that is made, the vocation that is graced through a new way of living. I suggest that this new way of living is not new at all but a model designed and practised throughout many centuries, a way of life called community. The Church in which our children are born, nurtured and loved, is the hope for this community.

This is a shared hope, one which seeks a corporate approach in the formation of the young. As the African proverb states, 'It takes a village to raise a child'[1] so the village needs to come alive for the child in the context of our contemporary, often individualistic setting. Rowan Williams has reflected on this need: 'Children are not brought up, are not educated or inducted into human society just by one or two people. The whole social complex of which they're a part makes them the persons they are'[2] The parish church structure which potentially informs a child's religious development faces many important challenges in welcoming, supporting and educating our young people. There are encouraging signs that this work is taking shape; that new levels of expertise are being applied not just 'in' church but across a broader landscape. However, the community or monastic model can inform our approach still further. Perhaps pilgrimage, journeying across the borderlands, is one way of arriving at this place called *metanoia*, a place of well-being which receives the child with openness and explores the vocation within, a place already described by Jo in the frontispiece of this book:

> There is a place we have not yet discovered. And yet, in our mind's eye, we have visited there again and again, working out its purpose, its parameters, its unlikely origins. When we speak of it, we do so tentatively, always somehow with an apology attached. It's hard to describe a place you have not found yet; to make believe a reality that apparently does not exist.
>
> This is a borderland place. Its identity is as yet unrealized. Calling us back to our roots, it is at once connected and connecting,[3] located in a landscape we both know and do not know, dislocated from any real knowledge of how our vision might come about. And yet the vision speaks of things real enough: repentance, renewal and transformation. People will go there, not because they have to but because they choose to, prepared to risk both joy and pain, discomfort and wonder.
>
> Over the years we have tried to run from our yearning, reminding ourselves of more sensible, realistic aspirations. But, each time we try to run, carrying our children with us, we find ourselves drawing back, turning round, returning to the point where we in fact we started out. Our identity is, and long since has been, bound up in this unknown vision. In time we hope it will shape and form us, that others will see it also and come to join us. It is, we hope, a place to which both we and others are travelling. Rightly or wrongly, we call this place *Metanoia*.

So how might one reach this place? What we have learnt so far is that to travel lightly is to travel well. One item that we have used and will need for our future passage, across the thresholds and the transitions, is the holy oil of Chrism. This is the pure oil of olives mixed with aromatic balsam. Chrism is used in each of the rites of baptism, confirmation and ordination. The tradition of anointing in religious ceremonies has continued from the time of Moses and throughout the Old Testament. Chrism is the oil which marks the coronation of kings, the consecration of high priests and the ordination of Levites, the priestly temple order. The Apostolic Fathers of the early Christian Church verified its usage for the sanctification of the Church and its people. So this ancient and sacred oil is a reminder, at one level, of the march of the people of faith. Today, the oil of Chrism is applied as a sacramental sign of God's grace working its purpose out in the anointed one. This is the oil that seals in the heart of the child the presence of the kingdom, it is the gift of the Holy Spirit. Those anointed in Chrism are therefore marked as *kingdom builders* with signs of divine grace. The Church believes that these are our kings and queens, our deacons, priests and bishops. These are our holy and sacred children, called by God in mind and spirit.

Gavin Knight, Pentecost 2009

Notes

Frontispiece

1   I have not been able to locate this exact phrase ('connected and connecting') but I certainly attribute the thought and theme to Esther de Waal – see *Living on the Border* (2001), as cited in the bibliography.

Introduction

1   This borderland territory has influenced writers and artists for generations and, most recently, has given rise to a series of books (the Borderland Series, published by Canterbury Press) in which different writers have drawn on different aspects of borderland country to consider faith from a variety of perspectives. These books were inspired by Ty Mawr Convent which, situated on the English–Welsh border, is just three miles from Monmouth. Both Ty Mawr and the writers who have drawn from it have served as an inspiration for the borderland theme of this book.

2   The same introduction is used for all books in the Borders series, but this particular citation is from the introduction to Esther de Waal's *Living on the Border* – see bibliography.

3   See <http://www.childrenssociety.org.uk/all_about_us/how_we_do_it/the_good_childhood_inquiry/report_summaries/13959.html>.

4   See <http://news.bbc.co.uk>.

5   6 February 2009.

6   2 February 2009.

7   *Church Times*, 17 July 2009.

8   See <http://www.yearofthechild2009.co.uk>.

9   This is taken from the well-known essay, 'Eight Stages of Man', printed in *Childhood and Society*, as cited in the bibliography.

10 Erikson's phrase 'a welcome trust of the community' also recalls the baptismal vows, which will be discussed in detail in chapters 3 and 4.

11 See Carter (2007); Hay with Nye (2006); Lamont (2007); Nye (2009); Richards and Privett (eds) (2009), as cited in the bibliography.

12 See pp. 38 and 284–285 of *Toxic Childhood* for examples, as cited in the bibliography.

13 This observation is made in an essay entitled 'The Vocation of the Child' which is one of a collection of essays in a book also entitled *The Vocation of the Child* (see bibliography).

Chapter 1

1 Jeremy Paxman made this comment in 2006 in his support for the English Heritage's initiative 'Inspired'. See <http://www.telegraph.co.uk/news/uknews/1518032/The-churches-that-are-praying-for-a-1bn-lifeline.html>. The citation can also be found in Pritchard (2007), p. 88, see bibliography.
2 This experience is described by the authors in detail in *Disturbed by Mind and Spirit: Mental Health and Healing in Parish Ministry* (2009).
3 In an Advent Retreat in 2005 at Lee Abbey, Father Simon Holden CR presented a session entitled, 'Landscapes of Life'.
4 Within this session (see previous footnote), Father Simon spoke about the 'landscape of memories'.

Chapter 2

1 For a discussion about the authorship of this work, see the Penguin introduction by Lewis Thorpe, as cited in the bibliography.
2 These questions are taken directly from the exhibition boards.
3 See Dallos and Draper (2005), as cited in the bibliography, for a comprehensive introduction to this vast field.

Chapter 3

1 See the work on the Dyadic Personality in Bruce Malina and Richard Rohrbaugh, full reference cited in the bibliography, pp. 112–113.
2 The seven sayings come from St John's Gospel, all NRSV translations: I am the bread of life (6:48); I am the light of the world (8:12); I am the gate for the sheep (10:7); I am the good shepherd (10:11); I am the resurrection and the life (11:25); I am the way, and the truth, and the life (14:6); I am the true vine (15:1).
3 Rowan Williams, from a homily given at Monmouth School, 11 March 2008, for the dedication and blessing of the Dewi Sant mosaic.
4 The theme of Jesus' obedience and the Father's authority is illustrated in Jane Williams' *Perfect Freedom*, see bibliography.
5 'The next day he saw Jesus coming towards him and declared, "Here is the Lamb of God who takes away the sin of the world! This is he of whom I said, 'After me comes a man who ranks ahead of me because he was before me.' I myself did not know him; but I came baptizing with water for this reason, that he might be revealed to Israel." And John testified, "I saw the Spirit descending from heaven like a dove, and it remained on him. I myself did not know him, but the one who sent me to baptize with water said to me, 'He on whom you see the Spirit descend and remain is the one who baptizes with the Holy Spirit.' And I myself have seen and have testified that this is the Son of God"' (John 1:29–34).

6   Pridmore (2008) cited in the *Church Times*, 4 July, 2008, p. 32 in an article entitled, 'Children as the Heavy-Laden'.
7   See Irenaeus' major work, *Against Heresies* (c. 180).
8   Isaiah 40:1–11, 45:2, 52:7; Malachi 3:1–6.
9   All citations from the liturgies of baptism, confirmation and ordination are taken from Common Worship (abbreviated to 'CW' from hereon). See bibliography for full reference.
10 The phrase 'sacred trust' echoes that used by the Good Childhood Inquiry.
11 Prayer over the water in the Liturgy of Baptism.
12 Prayer of Penitence, Liturgy of the Eucharist.
13 Common Worship, Initiation Services, Church House Publishing, London, 1998, p. 12

Chapter 4
1   Cited in chapter 3.
2   This and the two remaining psychological chapters will draw on various of Erikson's eight stages of development, as laid out in *Childhood and Society* (1950). For a discussion of the models, see Nye (2000b).
3   Research from different disciplines over decades, summarized in Sue Gerhardt's landmark book *Why Love Matters: How Affection Shapes a Baby's Brain*, is a painful but timely reminder that children's early experiences really are integral to their future development, and that early intervention is therefore critical.
4   Liturgy of Baptism.
5   Ibid.
6   This notion is derived from Winnicott's well-established idea of 'the good-enough mother': 'The good-enough mother … starts off with an almost complete adaptation to her infant's needs, and as time proceeds she adapts less and less completely, gradually, according to the infant's growing ability to deal with her failure' (Winnicott, 1953).
7   See Sue Gerhardt (2004) for an overview of these attachment styles.
8   This has already been discussed in chapter 3.
9   Since the 1960s it has been understood that the infant's role in initiating and regulating interaction with his mother is considerably greater than was once believed. The pattern of these interactions constitutes a cycle lasting approximately half a minute. Developmental researchers have recorded and identified different stages in the cycle, ranging from initiation (the moment when the child initiates contact with the mother) through to the peak of excitement (where a combination of behaviours might be present including the infant turning his head to face the mother, eye contact, smiling, a whole-body response with arms and legs, and vocalization). Importantly, the cycle ends with the baby's withdrawal from the interaction (i.e. looking away). The original research was carried out by Brazelton et al. (1974), cited by Douglas (2007) – see bibliography for full references.

10 Hazel Douglas founded the Solihull Approach and is author of
    Containment and Reciprocity (see bibliography). In her work, she
    brings together two concepts, containment (from the psychoana-
    lytical literature) and reciprocity (from the developmental literature).
    Her integrative approach was a significant influence on key compo-
    nents of this chapter.

11 E.g. 'Children Should be Heard in Church' (Jonathan Bartley, 18 July
    2008) and 'How Should Children Behave in Church?' (Giles Fraser,
    22 August 2008).

12 See *Working with Children, Adolescents and their Families: Third
    Edition* (2002) by Martin Herbert and Karen V. Harper-Dorton,
    Oxford: BPS Blackwell Publishing.

13 A paradoxical intervention (or task) can be defined as follows: 'the
    apparent encouragement of symptomatic or other undesirable
    behaviour [is used] in order to lessen such behaviour or bring it under
    control' (Weakland, Fisch, Watzlawick and Bodin (1974), cited by
    Dallos and Draper (2005), pp. 50–51).

14 *Church Times*, 15 May 2009.

15 Ibid., 1 May 2009.

16 The colour of this 'altar' cloth was changed throughout the Church
    year in accordance with the liturgical season.

17 'Godly Play ... is an imaginative approach to working with children,
    an approach that supports, challenges, nourishes and guides their
    spiritual quest ... [It] assumes that children have some experience
    of the mystery of the presence of God in their lives, but that they lack
    the language, permission and understanding to express and enjoy that
    in our culture' (Berryman, 2002a).

Chapter 5

1 This idea of 'a rite looking for a theology' comes from a comment
   made by Dominic Walker, Bishop of Monmouth.

2 Those candidates for confirmation who have not been baptized
   are baptized immediately before their confirmation.

3 This practice is not used universally in the Church. It was
   practised in the Roman Catholic Church for some time and has
   been adopted by some Anglican bishops, one of whom is Dominic
   Walker.

4 *Lectio divina* is best translated as holy reading, a meditative
   reflection upon Holy Scriptures.

5 The Liturgy of Confirmation.

6 From *Encyclical 84*, Michaelmas 2008.

7 Please see notes 3 and 4 to chapter 1.

8 *Festival Without End* is the title of Brother Roger's Journal
   1969–1970, Mowbray, Oxford, 1983.

9 The 'Today' programme on Radio 4, March 2009.

10 From 'The Byron Review: Children and New Technology', Press Release, 27 March 2008.
11 Commonly used translation from Rhigyfarch's *Buchedd Dewi*, his eleventh-century biographer.
12 Rowan Williams, 11 March 2008, Monmouth School.

Chapter 6

1 The middle childhood period varies somewhat in range in the literature. For the purpose of this book, I have defined the period according to Erikson's psychosocial stage model (see Carr, 2006). This coincides with the primary school years.
2 See Raikes and Thompson (2005), p. 57 for a fuller discussion.
3 Huston and Ripke, writing in the USA, define the middle childhood years as the period between ages six and twelve. While this range differs slightly from the criteria I have used, the principle is the same.
4 See <http://www.cofe.anglican.org/lifeevents/baptismconfirm/sectionc. html>.
5 See <http://www.naturalengland.org.uk/about_us/news/2009/020409. aspx>.
6 A useful introduction to cognitive behaviour therapy is: *An Introduction to Cognitive Behaviour Therapy: Skills and Applications* (2007) by David Westbrook, Helen Kennerley and Joan Kirk, London: Sage Publications.
7 See <http://www.childrenssociety.org.uk>.
8 This story was told on 'Sunday Half Hour', Radio 2, with Father Brian D'Arcy on 19 July 2009.
9 This response equates with the 'fight or flight' response, first described by Walter Cannon in the 1920s. It typifies two ways in which we are likely to respond to a stressful or anxiety-provoking situation.
10 Seeking to challenge and reshape existing beliefs is a key aspect of cognitive behaviour therapy.

Chapter 7

1 John Pritchard (2007) introduces the scheme of his book through the voice of a spiritual director to his colleague Jack Nicholls. The guidance was summarized as: 'the only thing he had to be concerned with as priest were the glory of God, the pain of the world and the renewal (repentance) of the Church' (p. x).
2 The Liturgy of Ordination.
3 The Liturgy of Ordination is not using 'family' and 'children' in a literal or exclusive sense, merely indicating the context of the called people, young and old, vulnerable and strong.
4 Phil Whiting, the artist, was commissioned to paint a series of compositions called *Places of Mourning in the Western World*. This series took the artist to Flanders, Oradour, Auschwitz-Birkenau, Ground Zero, and lastly to Srebrenica. It was in response to his visit to Bosnia in 2006 that

Whiting painted *Shoah* which formed part of the exhibition *Srebrenica: Paintings from the Grave.*

5   The phrase 'heart of darkness' is taken from the title of Joseph Conrad's book *The Heart of Darkness,* first published in 1899.

6   *The Tablet,* 11 July 2009, p. 15.

7   The Liturgy of Ordination.

8   Ibid.

9   Michael Mayne, Birmingham Ordination Retreat, 1999.

10   Exodus 20:2.

11   Gregory the Great (c. 540–604), in a letter to the Bishop of Marseilles, wrote about the importance of sacred images as a tool for educating the illiterate about their faith: 'who read in [the sacred images] what they cannot read in books ...'.

12   Dr Larry Culliford, Chairman of the Thomas Merton Society in Britain and Ireland and the founder of the special interest group Spirituality and Psychiatry, is cited in the *Tablet* by Elena Curtis, referring to the importance of stillness in our schools: 'Dr. Culliford talked about how some schools use a process called "stilling," in which the children have periods of meditation as part of the school day. Surveys had shown that it improved pupils' academic performance, behaviour and creativity' (*The Tablet,* 11 July 2009, p. 10).

Chapter 8

1   See Introduction to *The Blackwell Handbook of Adolescence* (2003), edited by G.R. Adams and M.D. Berzonsky, for more detail. This notes also that adolescence has its formal roots in the work by Granville Stanley Hall, *Adolescence: Its Psychology and Its Relations to Physiology, Anthropology, Sociology, Sex, Crime, Religion, and Education,* first published in 1904.

2   Erikson (1950/1995) was the first to name finding one's identity as the central task of adolescence.

3   See editors' Introduction to *The Blackwell Handbook of Adolescence,* which makes this statement regarding the situation in the USA.

4   Flyjacket of *Anne Frank: The Diary of A Young Girl: The Definitive Edition,* new translation by O.H. Frank and M. Pressler, London: Viking, 1997.

5   Cited in chapter 7.

6   Ibid.

7   See Rosenblum and Lewis (2003), as cited in the bibliography.

8   Winnicott's plea resonates with Rowan Williams' more recent reflections on childhood in *Lost Icons,* cited towards the end of chapter 4 in this book.

9   *Western Daily Press,* 19 February 2009.

10   Cited in chapter 7.

11   I would like to acknowledge Abbot Stuart Burns OSB for this thought. He once said to me many years ago that perhaps the most we can ever hope for is 'to want to want to be like Christ'.

Integrating Mind and Spirit (Part 4)
1   This echoes Winnicott (1971/1991), as discussed in chapter 8.

Epilogue
1   This proverb is cited in the report 'Being Adult about Childhood' – fuller reference detailed in note below.
2   The Archbishop of Canterbury's lecture to the Citizen Organising Foundation (COF) entitled 'Formation: Who's Bringing Up Our Children?' given at Queen Mary College, London, on Monday 11 April 2005 cited in *Being Adult about Childhood: A Consideration of The Good Childhood Inquiry. A Report from The Children's Society and the Mission and Public Affairs Division*, paragraph 130.
3   See note 1, Frontispiece.